Problems of the Islamic Republic of IRAN

BAHMAN AGHAI DIBA
PhD International Law

ISBN: 1461021979
ISBN-13: 9781461021971
Library of Congress Control Number: 2011907627

INTRODUCTION

The present collection of articles is aimed at making different aspects of life, politics and government clear in the Islamic Republic of Iran. Since its birth in 1979 the regime of the Islamic Republic of Iran has affected the life of the people living in Iran, in the region, and across the globe in a way that surprises many experts and ordinary people alike. They ask how come in the end of the twentieth century and beginning of the twenty first century, a regime can act so strangely, and not care about the national interests of the people that have created it and act against the ideals of the entire international community? After so many centuries, is this form of government the best that the Eastern culture and especially the Islamic world could produce? Is this their answer to problems of modern day statecraft?

The reality is that the Islamic regime of Iran is a unique creature produced by a certain segment of the Iranian society and it has imposed its will all over the country. The large majority of Iranians not only do not like this regime, but also do not share in the ideals pursued by the leaders of the Islamic Republic of Iran. In fact, looking at the regime in Iran and how it acts is a good lesson for future governments in Iran and other parts of the world (especially in the Islamic countries) to avoid doing as the Iranian regime does. This reminds me of the story of a character in Iranian history called Loghman.

"Loghman" was an Iranian philosopher in the ancient times. He was asked, "How did you get so polite and where did you learn your manners?" He said, "I learned from the impolite and ill-mannered persons. I stopped doing whatever they did." It seems that any government that wishes to be successful, serve its people in the best possible way, walk in the line of national interests and gain domestic and international recognition must pay attention to what the regime of the Islamic Republic is doing in Iran and refrain from those acts.

The articles of this collection try to introduce the problems of Iran as a country and see how the politicians of the Islamic Republic of Iran are tackling these problems. I think the most important message of this entire collection is that, for Iran , and probably for all other countries, a system of government based on strict religious rules, especially rules of Islam, does not work. Such a system is prisoner of its limitations, and contrary to the claims of the leaders of such regimes, it leads to injustice, mismanagement, corruption, war and conflict at domestic and international levels.

I take this opportunity to thank the special friend who suggested and took the first step for arrangement of the new edition of this collection, and also my fantastic editor that made the ideas mentioned in this collection clearer for the readers.

—Bahman Aghai Diba

TABLE OF CONTENTS

Misleading Words and Expressions in the Government and Politics of the Islamic Republic of Iran

When the leaders of the Iranian Islamic revolution came to Iran, they were talking about the democracy and human rights, people's rights, parliament, and so on. A great majority of the people in Iran, including and especially most of the elites and educated people did not understand the language of the religious Islamic personalities. The people of Iran and their elites were thinking that the mullahs and their theoreticians were talking about the words and expressions such as democracy and human rights in the same meaning as they had studied in the dictionaries of politics, academic books or observed in the Western countries. This misunderstanding cost the people of Iran dearly and the Iranians paid a high price for failing to see and understand the language of Mullahs. Due to the same misunderstanding, these words and phrases are often translated wrongly into other languages and you can see examples of these mistakes almost every day in the reports about the events of Iran in the domestic and foreign mass media.

Although the misunderstanding is so extensive that covers almost all political words and expressions in the Islamic Republic of Iran and many of these need clarification, I have chosen some of the most important ones to mention here:

1- Islam- These days many people have become interested to understand or introduce Islam as they see it themselves. This reminds me of one of the famous stories of people who had touched an elephant at night and they described the animal as the only part that they had touched. Almost all Muslims, and many non-Muslims when they are asked to comment, say that Islam is or is not something that they have in mind as true meaning of the religion. What is the truth? The truth is that all of them are right and all of them are wrong! What does this mean? If we understand that Islam is a collection of many different data, information, practices and ideas expressed in the form of the holy book and the practices of religious leaders (Imams, thinkers and believers) and scholars activities, then we can see that there are so many different interpretations of Islam. Probably the number of interpretations is equal to number of believers. Different lines of interpretation and thinking stem from the current necessities of times or circumstances. Ambiguity of main sources which is a common fact regarding all main religions of the world help to create more room for such interpretations. It is useless to read a line from Koran or refer to a practice of an Islamic leader to prove that Islam stands for one thing or the other. Many people belonging to various spectrums of social and political ideas express their own interpretation as the true expression of Islam while even they do not have the same terminology as others who do the same.

An example is the discussion about cutting the hand of thieves. Some Islamic sources say that the thief's hand should be cut under any circumstances and some other sources say that the cutting of thief's hand should be left to such time that an Islamic society is established (which has not yet taken place even in countries such as Iran or Saudi Arabia. In fact some sources believe that even the prophet Mohammad could not establish the ideal Islamic society in his time). Still another interesting example of diversity of interpretations is the enforcement of the Islamic punishment regarding "adultery". According to many well-known Islamic sources, adultery is proved only if five "qualified men" testify that they all have personally witnessed the whole process of unauthorized sexual intercourse. I do not think that you can find even one case which is compatible with such strict criteria but you can see that people are easily accused and punished by the so called Islamic courts for adultery.

Anyway, the bottom line is that almost all persons with any ideology from any part of the political and ideological spectrum from ultra right to the ultra left may find suitable materials in Islamic sources for their cause.

Some, like Ali Shairati create a self styled version of Islam and sell it to the historically illiterate youngsters of Iran and even an atheist ideology like communism finds allies in Islamic thought for its cause. The expression of "Marxist Islamic" is real, as strange as it may seem. The question "what does Islam say", unfortunately has no clear and common answer.

My mother was a religious person and she welcomed the change of regime in Iran (unlike my father who had studied the courses of being a mullah and left them to support the leftist trends), but when she saw the atrocities of the Islamic regime in Iran, she used to say: this is not Islam. I have heard this from many others in various levels inside and outside of Iran that this is not Islam. But if Khomeini, Khamenie, Rafsanjani and others who have spent their life to study the Islamic materials do not know what Islam is, then who is to say what is Islam?

My mother who could hardly read one page of Koran, or Jimmy Carter? (when Carter, the US President, protested to Khomeini and said that hostage taking was against Islam, Khomeini responded: I pray to Allah that Carter has become an interpreter of Islam too.) Is Islam what some Iranian and Arabs say, while disregarding all clear orders of Islam like the code of dress (one of the few things that a great number of Islamic sources and believers have in common and believe is mandatory) or what Osama Bin Laden is saying?

Is it what various Ayatollahs say in Iran (they do not agree on what Islam is. Some of those Ayatollahs have said in the past that if what the other Ayatollahs have said is the true interpretation of Islam, then they do not consider themselves as Muslim) or is it what the Islamic prayer leader said in the ceremony to honor the victims of terrorist acts in New York and Washington, held in the Washington Cathedral? Is it what some groups of people shouting anti-Western slogans in the streets of Cairo, Islamabad, Tehran, Jakarta and Nairobi say? The answer is again, they are all right and they are all wrong!

Islam says everything and Islam does not say anything. Fortunately, those who interpret Islam in a violent manner are a small minority, although they try to a show that they represent more than the reality. I conclude this section by saying that when the mullahs or quasi-mullahs like Ali Shariati say they want Islam, in fact they want the list of demands and they have filled the blanks themselves. Who says that people of a miserable country should follow the teachings of a person or persons who have filled the blanks arbitrarily? There are lessons in these for those who think. (The sentence is repeated so many times in Koran.)

2- Democracy- this word is used in the Islamic Republic of Iran to refer to a negative fruit of Western liberalism. "Government of the people by the people" is the worst thing that can happen in an Islamic theocracy based on the doctrine of "Velayte Faghigh" (Government of the Mullahs that claim to represent God).

However, due to the high respect that this word enjoys in the world and its popularity, the government of Iran sometimes uses an expression called "religious democracy" and usually even when they use the word "democracy" they mean "religious democracy". So, the expression "religious democracy" is per se an oxymoron.

At the moment there is a conflict between the Conservatives and the so-called Reformists in Iran on many issues. The Conservatives who have had the power during the last 30 years (do not get distracted by the false claims of Reformists to have any power in the main political decisions in Iran) believe that there is no place for democracy in a theocracy.

They are right. For the same reason, people of Iran and other Muslim countries should set aside the religious government in order to reach the democracy that they want for their country. Democracy is government of people and it has nothing to do with the government of God.

It is not even the dictatorship of the majority. Do not get distracted by use of this word by the mullahs and quasi-mullahs. What they have in mind is that the government belongs to God and he has transferred his power and privileges to the Mullahs and their herd-like followers. The religious persons are permitted to say any lies, deceive people, kill them and if necessary destroy masses of the people (even among themselves) to gain and keep the power vested in them by God. This reminds me of an article I read in Newsweek many years ago.

The article had a reference to the Masaie tribes in Africa. According to their religion God has created cows for Masaie, so the Masaie tribes attack other tribes, kill their men and women and children and bring cows to their tribes as acts of bravery and religious duty. When the governments question them about stealing others' cattle, they say we restore what belongs to us according to our religion.

3- Supreme leader (Valie Faghih)

This expression is usually taken as the Supreme Leader or some kind of king. It's not correct. "Vali" means guardian, or the person who has the position of guardian toward person or persons who need guardianship. According to the Iranian regime's version of Islam (or Sharieh), Valie Faghih is the person who has the guardianship over all Muslims who need the service. This has important direct and implied results.

The most important one is that those who are in need of guardianship are not qualified to appoint or elect the "guardian". Also, the guardian is not obliged to do things that the persons in need of guardianship (minors) want to be done. The minors are not entitled to make decisions for themselves and they are not in a position to question the acts of the guardian.

The guardian can tell lies or say one thing and do another because he is the sole source of distinguishing what is good or bad for the minors. However, according to the plan that mullahs in Iran have devised, and it has no real solid basis in Iran or anywhere else, a council of religious experts elects Valie Faghih. This council is the subject of another entry.

But it should be noted that the Supreme Leader is also considered as the deputy to the Valie Asr or Imam Zaman (Leader of present era). The Imam Zaman is the Islamic equivalent of Messiah. Nayebe Valie Asr, the title of the Supreme Leader, is in fact the divine connection of the leader. Whatever the Nayebe Valie Asr says is not only a personal interpretation of a religious figure, but also the result of his secret consultation with divine forces. I shall make a conclusion on this point: those who say what the leader of Iran says is not the law, are very wrong. The Leader's statements are more important and above the law.

4- Parliament- What we see in Islamic Republic of Iran is not the parliament in the Western dictionary of politics. Iran has an Islamic Consultative Assembly (Majlisse Shorae Islami). Islamic in this context means that the whole institution is subject to Islamic hierarchy. Consultative means that it is in the level of consultation and nothing more.

According to Islamic rules, Allah defines "laws" and mankind is not permitted to make laws, they can only find ways to implement them. Legislation is an act of God and approving anything contrary to those acts, is considered to be "Bedat" which means "initiative" and it is a major sin. As such there is no equivalent of the Western Parliament in the Islamic Republic of Iran.

The members of Majlis do not have political immunity for what they say and more important than that they are under no obligation to do or say what their constituents want, rather they are committed to act according to the interests of Islam (with official interpretation).

An "Islamic Assembly" cannot be a parliament and what we have in Iran, under the title of "Majles" is definitely not "legislative power." At the same time, "president" is not the head of the executive power, and the collection of mullahs who try to impose medieval laws on a modern society is not "judiciary" in the usual meaning of those expressions.

5- Judge

This word is usually taken as the equivalent of "Ghazi" in the Islamic Republic of Iran. This is not correct. What you find in the judicial system of the I.R. of Iran is "Hakeme Sharea" or "Ghazie Sharea". The fact that the complete name (Ghazie Sharea) is not usually used, and instead of that "Ghazi", which is the short form of those titles and individually means "Judge" is used, makes the issue confusing.

This is one of the very confusing words that the Islamic Republic of Iran likes and even persuades others in order to add to the complexity and then claim that the Westerners do not understand IRI's positions.

The Gahzie Sharea or Hakeme Sharea has unlimited discretion to decide disputes. No woman is allowed to have those titles. This personality is not required to observe the laws such as: constitutional law, civil law, criminal law, tax law, etc. He can judge according to his interpretation from religious laws or the views of well-known Islamic sources. Therefore, in the Islamic courts of the I.R. of Iran you can see texts of verdicts that say (for example): Mr. John Doe is convicted of committing so and so crime according to page 10 of chapter 11 of Imam Khomeini's "Resaleh of Towzih Al Masael" (the book containing the religious ruling of an ayatollah).

A judge has to be male, a religious expert, Shiia Ithna Asharieh (the brand of Shiia which believe in 12 Imams and the dominant branch of Islam in Iran) and he must have some other qualifications. It is clear that finding competent persons is a very difficult task, especially if you take into consideration that this kind of "competent" figures are in a position to get more lucrative positions in the government. The regime has appointed a great number of people in Iranian courts but these people are not real judges even though they hear the case and seem to issue verdicts, in reality, they only act as consultants to the "competent" judge behind the scene who may choose to check the work of the so-called appointed judges or not. Usually the competent judges end up signing hundreds of verdicts prepared by "incompetent" persons.

6- Election

All kinds of elections in the I.R .of Iran are held after detailed and strict screening of the candidates by several institutions. The aim of the screening is to make sure that the candidates are in the same line as the ruling circles. One of the important screening sources is the Guardian Council which will be introduced below.

There are others which work in different levels. The most important one in the second category is the Ministry of Intelligence (intentionally named as Ministry of Information in Iran to create confusion) which uses its own sources and also what it has inherited from the vast reports on a great number of people from SAVAK (Security organization of the former Shah of Iran). The results of these screenings usually lead to certain type of persons.

Most probable persons that come out of the screening are clergies and their relatives and/or employees of the Ministry of Intelligence. This is a known fact and people who do not have the required strong relations (by blood or marriage or through regular payment of a special tax called "the share of Imam") do not bother to become candidates. They know that there is no chance to pass the barrier and they save themselves the embarrassment.

Those who do not observe the rule, face the same result and they are eliminated without any regards to what people may think or what the reactions of other countries and organizations may be. Therefore, it can be said that there is no elections in the IR of Iran. What we have there is a kind of appointment. In the case of elections for Majlis, the supervisory organs reserve the right to reject the results of elections in at least two more stages.

7- Freedom(Azadi)

This word is largely misused in Iran. Some of the Iranian religious leaders claim that the freedoms which are mentioned in the Universal Declaration of Human Rights are not enough to express the scope of freedoms that Islamic regime gives to Human beings. If you review their teachings you will soon notice that they only use the term "human beings" to refer to their own followers, so they do not consider others as human beings. Therefore, only their followers are entitled to rights and privileges reserved for human beings.

8- Council of Experts

Majles-e Khobregan or Council of Experts has been introduced to people as a kind of constitutional assembly and it is referred to as such in the Western press. This not correct at all. Council of experts does not consist of people's representatives and it is not a "constitutional assembly" with powers to change the Constitutional Laws. The Council is a group of Mullahs who obey the orders of the Supreme Leader. They are all Mullahs screened by the "Guardian Council" for this post.

9- Guardian Council

It consists mostly of persons appointed by the Supreme Leader to keep an eye on the Majlis and elections. This is really interesting. If the state is really Islamic and its so-called parliament (Majles) is the Islamic Consultative Assembly, then why should another council supervise it to make sure that Islam is observed in the laws enacted by Majles? Who says that more than 300 persons (almost all of them Mullahs) who have been partly elected by the people (the reality is that even these persons are not people's representatives. The Guardian Council has strictly screened all candidates) do not understand Islam but the small group who gathers in the Guardian Council can do that? The Guardian Council has recently decided itself (through a conspiracy well-organized by the office of the Supreme Leader) that it has the authority to impose its decisions over the election process which is called Nezarate Estesvabi or interventionist supervision. The result has been a catastrophe in the government and politics of the Islamic Republic of Iran.

10- Expediency Council

The council was originally envisaged to solve the conflicts between the Majlis and the Guardian Council, but it is doing something else. The real name of this institution is: The "Assembly to Distinguish Expediency of the Regime". This is very clear. The council is not in charge of finding the expediency of Iran or Islam or anything like that. It is only in charge of finding what is best for continuation of the regime. This means that the council is permitted to say any lie, enter into any dirty tricks or violate any laws in order to protect the regime.

In fact, the Expediency Council (headed by Ayatollah Hashemi Rafsanjani) is trying to act as an institution under the Leader but above the government. However, the council has never done anything against the will and satisfaction of the Supreme Leader. The Expediency Council is just another tool of the tyrannical regime of the Islamic Republic of Iran as the last line of betrayal against the people of Iran and to perpetuate the regime that has lost its dubious legitimacy long ago.

MEANING OF "REVOLUTIONARY" IN THE ISLAMIC REPUBLIC OF IRAN

Revolutionary is a respected term in the Islamic Republic of Iran, but in reality after many years of the "revolution" whoever is revolutionary is in fact corrupt and a crook. In the early years of any revolution, the officials of the new regime, try to control the affairs through "revolutionary" methods and by "revolutionary persons" because they want to do many things in a short period of time and they feel that if they observe all the legal or even customary standards and go through the logical process, they may lose the main game. Therefore, "revolutionary" acts are a kind of temporary and limited actions taken by the new regime until the affairs return to their normal conditions and then they go back to observe logic, standards, due processes, laws and so on. It is not acceptable for a regime like the Islamic Republic of Iran, after a quarter century of dominance over the country, to still speak of revolutionary persons, institutions, practices and so on. Therefore, the expression of "revolutionary" in Iran is a reference to violation of laws and standards and due process.

The Islamic revolutionary courts that were established in the early years of the so-called Islamic revolution were aimed at rapid trial of the persons that the new regime considered as enemies. These courts condemned thousands of people to death without observing any laws. They have claimed on various occasions that they enforced the Islamic codes.

However, in reality they have only enforced the views of the ruling circles disguised as Islamic codes. It is notable that starting from the first Islamic revolutionary courts up to now, no prominent Islamic clergy has accepted to be a judge or a high-ranking official in the Islamic revolutionary courts. These courts are full of young and ambitious clergies who owe their positions and promotions only to the obedience to the ruling circles.

These courts claim to be "revolutionary" in the sense that they do not have the time and patience of observing the existing laws and legal procedures. They make their decisions based on strange sources such as: the "personal view of the Islamic Judge", the religious rulings of important sources of Taqleed (imitation) in the Shiite-Islamic society, and especially the Resaleh (book of the Islamic rulings) of Ayatollah Khomeini. This means that a judge may condemn a person to death, or a lesser punishment with reference to a certain page of the Resaleh of Ayatollah Khomeini.

Although this practice was unacceptable even in the early years of the "revolution" (due to contradiction to the Universal Declaration of the Human Rights, the International Convention on the Civil and Political Rights, and the International Convention on the Social and Economic Rights, that all of them are ratified by Iran and even without ratification, they are part of the laws in force for all states in the world), After many years of the so-called revolution, what is the need for such courts?

The "revolutionary" courts are per se in violation of due processes, implementation and enforcement of the laws and they are a symbol of "lawlessness" and double standard. How is it possible to have two legal systems in one country? This legal chaos has not only violated the rights of Iranian citizens, they have been the reason the foreign sources are reluctant to tackle (or invest) in Iran.

The foreign companies that are active in Iran have in fact concluded agreements with the government that takes the possible conflicts of the two sides out of the jurisdiction of the Iranian courts and makes them dependent on international arbitration and other forms of international litigation. This is what "revolutionary" court means in Iran. In order to reform the system, the revolutionary courts must be eliminated and many of the cases that they have tried must be retried according to internationally acceptable laws and legal procedures.

The institutions, such the Bonyade Mostazafan (the Foundation for the Deprived), Bonyade 15th of Khordad, the Charity Foundation of Imam Khomeini, and countless other institutions that are collectively called "revolutionary institutions" are in fact centers for the activity of the ruling circles in the Islamic Republic of Iran, without observing the laws of the land or as a matter of fact any law; for example, these institutions give loans to the herd-like followers of the regime, pay huge amounts of money to the clergies, send money for terrorist organizations in various countries, organize and operate their own systems of accounting (they do not pay taxes), have their own ports of importation and exportation without paying due taxes to customs officials, do not get inspected by the legal authorities, recruit thousands of people without observing national laws, send students to universities without students having to pass the difficult university entrance examination, buy, sell, and produce whatever they wish without observing any regulations, getting permits and licenses and so on. In short, the "revolutionary" institutions in the Islamic Republic of Iran are the centers for corruption and complexes of the official organized criminal activities.

"Revolutionary" persons are considered as qualified persons for all positions in the Islamic Republic of Iran. Whenever there is a discussion in the Majles, media, government and so on, they are "looking for revolutionary persons for the jobs". However, revolutionary persons at the moment are the most unqualified persons for any post. The "revolutionary persons" do not observe laws, do not consult with others, impose their own views as if they are the single most important reference point on any issue (ironically they usually are least qualified), and do not care about criticisms (even if the criticism is justified) are the worst choice for any job. In fact, most of the "revolutionary" managers of the Islamic Republic of Iran must stand trial for their illegal actions.

All those who speak about returning to the earlier years of the Islamic revolution (including and especially the new "revolutionary" president of Iran), mean they do not want to observe even what they have set as laws. They want to be free to take any action that they desire under the pretext of being revolutionary. In a nutshell, any person who calls himself "revolutionary" in the present regime of Iran is in fact "counter-revolutionary" even by the standards of the current regime.

IRAN IS IN SERIOUS DANGER

The Islamic regime has put Iran in danger of war, destruction and disintegration. While almost all countries in world had good years of development, Iran has become closer to misery, poverty, starvation, sanctions, war and underdevelopment.

Iran has not succeeded to improve its economy. Despite the increasing oil prices, most of Iran's income has been spent by the Iranian regime for enrichment of Mullahs and their lackeys, helping the Palestinian extremists, the Syrian crooks, the terrorists in Iraq, and the Hizbollah in Lebanon.

The people of Iran are witnessing that their national wealth is plundered not by occupying forces, invading enemies, but by the Mullahs who do not care about the national interests and do not care about the people of Iran. In fact, the Mullahs of the Iranian regime do not consider those who defy them as human beings.

It is a cause of great embarrassment for the people of Iran that the Islamic regime of Iran is acting against the national interests of this country in one of the most sensitive eras of the history of the world. The destruction caused by the Mullahs in Iran will not go away for a long time. Iran is in need of a long period of purification.

The people of Iran are not able to change or reform their regime. The experience of reforms has failed. Now it's time for regime change. Iranians are well aware of the corruption and inefficacy of the regime of Iran. I have been taking part in many programs in the Iranian TV and radio stations out of Iran and in many cases I have been the guest of the programs that accept direct calls from Iran. In numerous cases the people in Iran have called and said that they do not need me or others to explain for them the extent of violation of human rights or corruptions of the regime in Iran.

The people of Iran are already feeling and experiencing these crimes directly and in the flesh. They want to know what can be done to get rid of this regime and its agents and how this nation can be saved. What are you going to do about it? Is the US going to confront this regime seriously? Are the Iranians in opposition groups out of Iran able to do something other than attacking and humiliating reach other and blaming each other for the prolongation of the Islamic regime in Iran?

This has given me a sense that almost all of the Iranian people are waiting for the outside powers to come to the conclusion that it is not possible to live with a regime like the one that is stationed in Iran and by its corrupt and oppressive policies has in effect taken its people hostage.

Why are so many Iranians looking outside to the opposition groups out of the country and the foreign powers? The answer seems to me as follows:

Something in the conscious of the Iranians, at least for the last couple of centuries, says that nothing will happen here, except those orchestrated by outside powers. Whenever you talk to many Iranians about the situation of Iran, they listen to whatever you say and then they take a deep breath and say: "of course, all depends on what the British or the Americans or the Russians want." According to these Iranians "not even a leaf falls from a tree in Iran, without the foreign hands knowing it."

This feeling of futility of struggle against powerful foreign hands that hold the regime of Iran sends a strong signal of frustration all over the Iranian society. It is a common thing in Iran that when the Regime of Iran does something against the interests of the county or in violation of human rights or a serious case of corruption, the people of Iran (including many educated persons) curse "the British and the Americans" instead of the Mullahs of Iran, because they think the Mullahs are such miserable elements that are not even worth talking about. It is the foreign hands that have made these anti-Iranian elements dominant over the fate of this country. It is the foreign hands that want Iran to be poor and devastated and Mullahs (intentionally or unintentionally) are their instruments. Therefore until such time that these foreign hands (the British and the Americans) let the regime go, there is no way to fight it.

2- The Iranians seriously doubt that the Western powers (including and especially) the USA, are sincere in their opposition to the Iranian regime. They argue that the Islamic Republic was brought to power and kept in power by the Western countries because they wanted to follow the policy of containment of communism with the Green Belt (green for the flag of Islam). The Islamic Republic has many advantages for the Western countries (the colonial powers) such as: mismanagement and corruption of the Iranian regime leaves a lot of space for the Western powers to exploit. They control the resources of Iran especially oil. They make the rich sheikhdoms of the Persian Gulf afraid of the Iranians in order to sell them all kinds of arms. They keep a big country like Iran backward and stop the development in Iran so that the people of this country are always in need of the products of the Western countries. An important proverb in Iran is that "the British colonial powers were convinced that in order to control the Arabs they should keep the Arabs well-fed and in order to control the Iranians, they should keep the Iranians hungry."

3- The Iranians are clearly dissatisfied with the treatment that the European countries are showing towards the regime of Iran. The EU countries are competing with each other to have better relations with Iranian regime. The Italian government recently protested to the fact the only three European Countries (France, the UK and Germany) were negotiating with Iran regarding the nuclear case of Iran and they demanded to be added to the negotiating team. To many Iranians, the move of the Italian government was not aimed at solving the nuclear case of Iran but to get better chances of access to the lucrative deals with the Iranian government. A look at the level of the transactions of the EU-3 with the Iranian regime supports this idea.

4- The Iranians inside Iran are attaching much importance to the opposition out of Iran because they think these groups are closer to the powers that determine the future of the Iranian regime. At the same time, the pattern by which Khomeini came to Iran (going to Paris and getting support of the West and flying to Tehran with Air France, while the French captain was holding his hand and especially the fact that when Khomeini came to Iran, the government was still under the control of the existing system.) gives the people of Iran a clear indication about the extent of foreign involvement when fundamental change happens in Iran.

6- The Iranian people are also faced with the problem of finding an alternative to the Iranian regime. There is no clear alternative to the regime. The opposition groups are very weak and disorganized and they have not succeeded to get the trust of the Iranian people.

Human Rights in the Islamic Republic of Iran: Contradiction of Universal Standards with Dominant Ideology

The United Nations General Assembly (UNGA) expressed its serious concern about the violation of human rights in the Islamic Republic of Iran in a resolution adopted on 16th of December 2005. The UNGA's resolution has referred to:

- Harassment, intimidation of the human rights defenders, non-governmental organizations, political opponents, religious dissenters, journalists and students.

- Restriction of the freedoms of assembly, press, and expression,

- Arbitrary arrests and detentions,

- Disqualification of a large number of candidates in the elections,

- Torture, inhumane and degrading treatment and punishments, public executions, execution of the people under 18 years of age, amputation, flogging and stoning

- Violation of the rights of women,

- Violation of the rights of the religious and ethnic minorities, including Christians, Jews, other sects of Islam, and Bahai's.

This is not the first time that the United Nations has condemned the violations of human rights in the Islamic Republic of Iran and asked for changing the policies of the regime. During the last 30 years, the United Nations has, at least 20 times, adopted such measures in the framework of its non-binding decisions (only the decisions of the Security Council of the United Nations under certain chapters of the UN Charter are mandatory and binding on the member states). However, the laws and practices of the dominant regime have not changed and recently they have become even worse.

The regime of Iran has called the resolutions of the UNGA as "unacceptable" and has rejected the resolutions as foreign interference in the domestic affairs of Iran and alien propaganda. Therefore, one should not expect that the new resolution of the UNGA affects the behaviors of the regime any more than the previous ones.

The main reason for this is the contradiction of the universal standards of the human rights (as reflected in the Universal Declaration of the Human Rights, the International Convention on Civil and Political Rights, and the International Convention on Social and Economic Rights) with the basic policies and the religious ideology of the regime. They cannot stop the current policies and start observing the internationally recognized standards of human rights and fundamental freedoms, as long as they observe the ideological guidelines of the regime based on the interpretation of Islam by certain Mullahs.

In fact asking the regime of the Islamic Republic of Iran to observe these rights is asking them to close shop. Because, the regime owes its existence to these religious guidelines, the ruling circles in the Islamic Republic of Iran do not care how their practices differ from universal standards of decency and humanity. In fact, the Mullahs see the disparity as the reason for their "superiority and nobility" among the countries in the world and they invite other countries to copy them in order to be "saved" from the scourge of the Western liberalism and communism.

Let us take the case of elimination of discrimination against women (these are only some of the cases of the discrimination against women in the law and practice of the Islamic Republic of Iran: women's share of inheritance is half of men's. Men have an absolute right to divorce while women do not. The right of child custody is always with men. Women are not allowed to travel without direct permission of their husbands or male supervisors.

A woman's testimony in court is worth half of a man's. Women are not allowed to be judges. Also, according to the dominant version of Islam in Iran, in case of changing the religion from Islam to anything else (Ertedad), men are immediately condemned to death, but women are imprisoned and beaten several times every day during the daily prayers five times a day until they give up the new religion and return to Islam).

These cases are against the UN standards of the Human rights (especially the United Nations Convention on Eradication of all kinds of Discrimination Against Women). However, they exist because they reflect the dominant version of Islam in Iran. The regime believes it has a "divine" duty to implement these actions and practices. What is the use of asking them to stop? The regime exists to do these.

This is their Reason D'eter (the cause of existence). The religious dictatorship that controls Iran cannot afford to accept freedom of expression, religion and so on. What is the use of advising these figures to observe the freedom of religion? The criminal codes of Iran include certain types of criminal acts that you cannot find in any judicial system in the world. Killing gays and children are some of them.

While the civilized world is moving towards "decriminalization" (reducing the number of acts that put people in prisons), the Islamic Republic of Iran is expanding the definition of criminal conduct to include what was not previously criminal. Young people are beaten and flogged and even killed for drinking a couple of beers and getting together with friends of the opposite sex.

The Prisons are lawless territories. In fact, the Bylaw of Iranian Prisons is an illegal text created by the former Butcher of Evin (Assadolah Lajevardi) that had imposed the text on the judiciary without going through legal process.

The text of the Bylaw lacks many of the important elements of the UN standards about the treatment of prisoners and administration of justice.

Bahai's are one of the religious minorities who have been facing many restrictions, discriminations and improper treatments and even arbitrary arrest and execution in Iran. It is not acceptable in a country like Iran that certain number of people are prosecuted, set aside from jobs, and stopped from going to school and imprisoned solely because they have certain religious beliefs. This is an embarrassment for the entire Iranian nation. However, the Islamic Republic of Iran feels a special hostility toward the followers of the Bahai Faith because they have their own interpretations of certain religious points.

The adoption of the new resolution by the UNGA is not totally useless. In the past the Human Rights Commission of the United Nations had designated special reporters for the violation of human rights in Iran. During the last years of Khatami, the commission did not do so in the hope that the regime was showing signs of reforms. Now that the new resolution of the UNGA is adopted and the new institution called the Human Rights Council (one of the results of the recent conference of the Heads of States of the UN members for reforming the United Nations) has been created, the issue of the human rights violation in Iran is one of the first items on its agenda and hopefully they will designate a new special reporter for the Islamic Republic of Iran in the same field. This issue may also affect the referral of the nuclear case of Iran to the UNSC.

The reasons for adoption of the resolution on violation of human rights in the Islamic Republic of Iran at the present juncture are:

1- The case of Dr. Zahra Kazemi, the Canadian-Iranian photojournalist who was killed under mysterious conditions while she was arrested in Iran in 2003 - Her death and reluctance of the Iranian authorities to return her body to the Canadian or impartial authorities despite the request of her son and the fact that her mother admitted that Iranian authorities had put pressure on her for the quick burial of her daughter, coupled with the reports about the case mistrial as well as the remarks of an Iranian physician who was working in the hospital where Dr. Zahra Kazemi was taken about Zahra being beaten, tortured and possibly raped in the Evin Prison, all led to a new wave of actions by the Canadian officials to follow the human rights violations in Iran. They first took the case of these violations to the Third Committee of the UNGA and now the plenary session of the UNGA has passed the new resolution.

2- The remarks of the new president of Iran regarding denial of the Holocaust and asking for removal of Israel from the world map.

3- The policies of the new government in the line of making Iranian government more fundamentalist, religiously conservative and extremist in the area of foreign policy.

4- The end of hope in the reforms introduced during the government of the former president (Khatami). In fact Khatami and his followers never had real power during the 8 years that they wasted. The main strings of power were always under the control of the extremist elements and the Mafia of power in Iran (led by the so-called Supreme Leader). The government of Khatami had created a kind of hope for some reforms inside and outside of Iran. Attention of Khatami to issues like "Dialogue among the Civilizations" (apparently he had proposed this in lieu of the idea presented by Huntington about the Clash of Civilizations) had made some people hopeful that the Mullahs of Iran (who had usually opposed all signs of civil society) might eventually be able to throw away some of the gibberish of Khomeini and start practicing some "civilized" approaches. However, the failure of Khatami proved these hopes to be in vain. It seems that the international community, like the people of Iran, is reaching the point of understanding that the only way to observe human rights in Iran is toppling the regime of the Islamic Republic of Iran which is the enemy of human rights inside and outside of Iran.

Iran Oil Bourse and Petrodollar Wars

For several years, a plan for establishment of an oil exchange center under the title of "Iran Oil Bourse" (IOB) has been under discussion. (1) The most important point about the plan is that it wants to replace dollar with euro for the currency that is used for oil transactions. Some sources have claimed that the US is so sensitive to this move against the dollar that it is going to attack Iran before the IOB starts working. These sources claim that the same issue instigated the US attack against Iraq.

I think at the present conditions and under the control of the Islamic Republic of Iran, the IOB will neither be a real source of threat for anyone nor a source of interest for Iran. The government of the Islamic regime of Iran, as an inefficient, unpopular, undemocratic, anti-human rights, corrupt, non-transparent, illogical (ignoring the national interests and defending the hardliner religious zealots all over the world), un-elected, tyrannical, mismanaged and isolated government which is hostage to the religious ideology of the Arabs of 1400 years ago, is not able to start such a plan. At the same time, the engineers of the conspiracy theories of "petrodollar wars" are neglecting (probably intentionally) many important issues in this case. Most of these theories are based on false assumptions.

The Iranian oil Bourse will not be able to make any changes in the oil market and it is not able to do anything important against the dollar. Countries like Russia, China, Europe and many others are not so naïve to wait until a corrupt and inefficient system like the Islamic Republic of Iran makes a change that they like. If they were interested in doing something like this (changing the dollar base with euro for oil transactions), they would have done it long before. There were several attempts, including by Putin in Russia and the UAE for doing this and they were stopped due to the existing difficulties.

No country or reputable company is ready to establish a brokerage unit for oil (as matter of fact for anything else) in the Kish Island of Iran and put its personnel and establishment subject to the jurisdiction of the revolutionary courts of Ira, or the illegal acts of the disciplinary forces of the Iranian regime or the irresponsible actions of the "organized thugs" called Basijees.

What is the petrodollar wars? Hadi Zamani (2) in his informative and detailed series of articles about the Iranian Oil Bourse (written in Persian and posted consecutively in http://news.gooya.com) has mentioned: "According to the theory of petrodollar wars, the monopolistic situation of dollar for the foreign exchange reserves of the world imposes a great burden over all countries... It allows the USA to continue to have its structural economic imbalance and lets it keep its hegemony over the international economy.... therefore keeping the status of dollar is at the top of the foreign policy priorities of the United States. At the moment, due to the risks and dangers that threaten the status of dollar, the US is following a militaristic policy in the Middle East region in order to stop the collapse of its economic, political and military hegemony.... on the basis of the arguments related to the petrodollar wars, the reason for US attack against Iraq... was not combat against international terrorism or stopping Iraq from getting nuclear weapons. The US aim was keeping the hegemony over the international economy. For the same reason, immediately after the occupation of Iraq, the US officials ordered the oil transactions of Iraq back to the dollar system...".

Professor Krassimir Petrov (3), from the American University in Bulgaria (his article on this subject has been used by countless sources and websites as an academic argument for the validity of petrodollar wars theory) writes: "... Bush's war in Iraq was not about existing weapons of mass destruction, about defending human rights, about spreading democracy, or even about seizing oil fields. It was about defending the dollar, ergo the American Empire; it was about setting an example that anyone who demanded payment in currencies other than U.S. Dollars would be likewise punished...The Iranian government had proposed to open an Iranian Oil Bourse...If this happens...The Europeans will not have to buy and hold dollars in order to secure their payment for oil, but would instead use their own currency. The Chinese and the Japanese will be especially eager to adopt the new exchange. It will allow them to drastically lower their enormous dollar reserves and diversify them with Euro... The Russians have economic interest in adopting the Euro... Russians have also revived their nationalism; if embracing the Euro will stab the Americans, they will gladly do it and smugly watch the Americans bleed. The Arab oil-exporting countries will eagerly adopt the Euro as a means of diversification against rising mountains of depreciating dollars. Should the Iranian Oil Bourse gain momentum and accelerate, the interests that matter...will eagerly adopt the Euro, thus sealing the fate of the dollar. Americans cannot allow this to happen, and if necessary, will use a vast array of strategies to halt or hobble the exchange's operations: Sabotaging the exchange, coup d'etat, Negotiating acceptable terms, joint UN war resolution, unilateral nuclear strike, and unilateral total war.[this section is made brief]"

Jerome R. Corsi (4) has stated in his writings: "Iran and Venezuela have joined forces in an effort to undermine the U.S. dollar. In October 2005, Venezuelan President Hugo Chavez announced that Venezuela was ready to move the country's foreign-exchange holdings out of the dollar and into the Euro. He also called for the creation of a South American central bank designed to hold, in Euros, all the foreign assets."

Also, Mike Whitney (5) in his article dated Feb. 4 2006 claims: "Many war-weary news hounds are probably wondering why Russia caved in at the IAEA board meeting and agreed to have Iran sent before the UN Security Council... Obviously, Russia's foreign minister's comment that the referral to the UNSC is "only a warning" doesn't adequately explain why Russia would have placed its ally in such grave danger of a preemptive attack. It may be, in the words of the Godfather, that the Bush administration made Putin "a deal he couldn't refuse". For one thing, most news reported that "Lukoil will replace the disgraced Halliburton" in providing fuel in Iraq...The truth is, that even the control of oil is not nearly as critical to the US as maintaining its continued dominance in the exchange of oil in greenbacks. If Iran is allowed to open its oil bourse (exchange) and openly compete with the US's monopoly on trading oil in petrodollars, the central banks across the globe will dump hundreds of billions of dollars overnight and the American economy will disappear beneath the waves."

In his other article, Mike Whitney (6) has added: "...The [US] administration has no hope of securing the votes needed for sanctions or punitive action. The trip to the Security Council [of the Iranian nuclear case] is purely a ploy to provide the cover of international legitimacy to another act of unprovoked aggression... We should now be focused on how Washington intends to carry out its war plans, since war appears to be inevitable. Bush has no intention of occupying Iran. Rather, the goal is to destroy major weapons-sites, destabilize the regime, and occupy a sliver of land on the Iraqi border that contains 90% of Iran's oil wealth. Ultimately, Washington will aim to replace the Mullahs with American-friendly clients who can police their own people and fabricate the appearance of representative government. But, that will have to wait. For now, the administration must prevent the incipient Iran bourse (oil-exchange) from opening and precipitating a global sell-off of the debt-ridden dollar..."

The answers to the theory

Paul Craig Roberts has written " readers keep asking if Bush is attacking Iran because it plans to open an oil bourse that would permit oil to trade in Euros.... the answer is no.... the dollar's value depends on the world's willingness to hold dollar denominated assets, not on the currency used to pay oil bills." (7)

Once again looking at the articles of Hadi Zamani on the subject makes many points clear. He writes in the articles mentioned earlier that: "...those who oppose this doctrine argue [I have put the reasons that Zamani has mentioned in numbers and changed some words accordingly]:

1- This doctrine exaggerates the status of dollar for the US economy.

2- The doctrine is ignoring the elements that have resulted in the present role of dollar as the reserves currency in the world and costs of staying in such a position.

3- The euro is not able to tolerate the costs of being a currency for exchange reserve and the European countries are not ready for such a burden.

4- This doctrine is not taking into consideration the realities and complex mechanisms of the oil market.

5- The doctrine is based on several handpicked evidences and it degrades the functions of the global economy into several conspiracies.

6- The first reason for the present role of dollar as the dominant currency in exchange reserves is the power of the American economy, not political conspiracies. The US produces almost one third of the gross global products.

7- In the long run, dollar has more stability as compared to the other currencies.

8- Transferring the euro into the currency for the global reserves will increase its value 20 to 40 percent, and such an increase will weaken the exports of the euro countries considerably. The European economy is not powerful enough to tolerate such a pressure.

9- There is no serious indication that the countries of the world, including the oil exporting countries are ready to accept a euro based oil market. Since 1986 the oil prices are determined according to complex tables and spot changes in the New York and London exchange markets (called New York Mercantile Exchange, or NYMEX and International Petroleum Exchange or IPE correspondingly.)

10- OPEC countries are not ready to change the basis for oil transactions so easily. OPEC has tried several times to change the basis for the oil prices to euro, or Special Drawing Rights (SDRs of the IMF) or a basket of currencies and each time it has been abandoned.

The plan for establishment of Iranian Oil Bourse was first put on the table in 2000... The IOB will include petrochemical products and gas too. In the initial phase the transactions does not include crude oil (perhaps up to three years). Later it will include all oil transactions including the swap operations of the Caspian Sea oil. According to the claims of the Iranian government the IOB will turn into a major oil transactions center in the Middle East. The transactions will be in Euros and the monopoly of dollar over the global oil markets will end.

However, entering this business requires reform and preparation in the economic, legal and administrative structure of the country. At the moment due to the following limitations, Iran cannot work in an international oil bourse:

*Iran lacks proper financial, banking, insurance, customs, commercial structures, proper tax laws,

* Iran's oil sector is under the dominance of the governmental sector,

* Iran lacks competition in market,

*Iran is not able to attract foreign investment

* Iran lacks necessary expert manpower, necessary advanced technology, electronic commerce structure, necessary economic, legal and technical infrastructures, system of the credit cards in global level, commercial customs,

*Iran is still not a member of the World Trade Organization (WTO),

*Iran is already under American sanctions,

*Iran is not in a proper situation in the global economy,

*Iran has to observe the OPEC quotas,

* The IOB is based on the market being good for the producers, but the fluctuations in the oil prices may put the participating countries in a difficult situation.

Zamani adds an important point for those who care about the religious aspects of the IOB and he says, "It seems that the IOB is against the religious rules of Islamic Shari'a in Iran. The IOB faces problems based on the Islamic jurisprudence limitations and stumbling blocks...oil bourse is in fact a future market. One of its aims is to reduce risks of the oil transactions.... according to the studies of the Iranian experts, the mechanism of future oil bourse transactions is basically contrary to the Islamic jurisprudence of the Islamic Republic of Iran (please refer to the article in Persian by Hojatolislam Ghanimi Fard, and Mohammad Aram Bonyar in the site of Imam Sadegh University regarding the "Feasibility Study of the Establishment of the Oil Bourse by the Islamic Republic of Iran)." Zamani concludes: "The success of the oil bourse depends on transparency of the economic structure and rationalization of the Iranian foreign policy." (8)

Also, Colin Nunan has written in the Energy Bulletin "...However, others have claimed that the idea that the currency in which oil is sold matters at all is based on a poor understanding of economics...Those arguing that the denomination of sales is crucial to dollar strength have tended to say that countries are forced to save dollars so that they have dollars to buy oil. Their critics, however, reply that you do not have to save in dollars to buy oil since you can save in whichever currency you want and then buy dollars on the foreign exchange market whenever you want to buy oil. What matters, say the critics, is in which currency people ultimately save rather than in which currency they trade...So can we conclude that an Iranian oil bourse trading oil in Euros is the real reason for the current crisis? Perhaps this is prematurely jumping to conclusions... I have yet to see a clear statement on this from the Iranian government." (9)

The IOB is a good idea. In the hands of a proper Iranian government that establishes good relations with many countries, including and especially the USA. It could turn, in the long run, into a profitable center. The present day Iran lacks the necessary preparations for such a move. Even if taking steps for such reforms are started today, it will take some time to make the necessary grounds ready. However, the government of the Islamic regime of Iran is not even walking in the direction of those reforms. Unfortunately the IOB is a stillborn.

Notes and references:

(1) According to the official Mehr News Agency in Iran: "Iran is to form joint oil brokerage as the reputable international stock exchanges like London, New York and Singapore." (http://www.payvand.com/news/05/nov/1248. html, dated 11/27/2005)

(2) http://news.gooya.com/world/archieves/039259.php dated 11/29/2005

(3) http://www.freemarketnews.com/Analysis/183/3744/2006-02-10.asp?nid=3744&wid=183   dated 2/10/2006.

(4) http://worldnetdaily.com/news/printer-friendly. asp?ARTICLE_ID=48751, dated 2/11/2006.

(5) http://www.opednews.com/maxwrite/print_friendly. php?p=opedne_moke_whi_060204_wh..., dated 2/11/2006

(6) http://www.jihadunspun.com/intheatre_internal. php?article=106112&list=/home.php, dated Feb.4, 2006

(7) http://www.vdare.com/asp/printPage.asp?url=http:// adare.com/roberts/060210_oil.htm

(8) http://news.gooya.com/world/archieves/040054.php dated 11/29/2005 (9) http://www.energybulletin.net/print. php?id=12463 dated 30 Jan.2006

TURNING IRAN
INTO A SUICIDE BOMB

During the last couple of years, the most important countries of the world have expressed their dissatisfaction about various program and policies of the Islamic Republic of Iran. The most important case is the nuclear issue of Iran, but the cases of contention do not end there. There are problems about human rights, international terrorism, the Middle East peace process, export of Islamic revolutionary tactics, persuading the extremist elements, teaching religious intolerance, violation of the international norms and so on.

In almost no case, the regime of Iran has accepted the views of the international community and especially those of the most important countries of the world. Most of the countries in the world do not dare even to oppose the USA and the EU verbally. The Islamic regime challenges all policies and even the civilization and ways of living of the Western countries. The Iranian regime's officials keep calling the Western state's most important officials idiots and retarded people that tell lies and do not understand the Islamic ideology and what Islam does for the people of the Muslim countries.

Therefore this question comes to mind: what makes the Islamic regime of Iran feel so powerful and even arrogant? Is it military power? Has it got nuclear bombs hidden in places that nobody knows (not even the MKOs who have revealed most of the secret nuclear programs of the Iranian regime in the past)? What does the regime of Iran rely on? How do they manage to live like this? Is the Hidden Imam behind the Iranian regime? The officials of the Islamic Republic, since Khomeini, have said many times that Imam-e Zaman or the Hidden Imam (the Islamic-Shiite Messiah) was backing the regime of Iran. Iranian officials have called Iran: "the country of Imam-e Zaman". (Refer to the related article in this collection)

Some of the people who do not have serious religious convictions have been wondering: the Iranian regime is so corrupt and its officials are so naïve and illiterate and the level of management is so low that the continuation of the Islamic regime is a source of astonishment. They keep asking themselves: Perhaps the Imam-e Zaman is really backing this regime (or some other hidden hand. Some people, including many of the educated Iranians see the hidden hand as the hand of the British or even the Americans), otherwise how on earth is it possible that such a corrupt and inefficient regime stand on its feet for so many years and even take a step further and defy the demands of the important powers of the world so arrogantly?

The big powers of the world have been able to change many things in the world in the past and present with a spectrum of tools, starting from a mere declaration of intent to full military operations. How come then a country with small population, underdeveloped economy, unemployment rate of 30 percent, fifty percent of the population under 30 years old, dependent fully on the outside world for almost everything, including food, raw materials and industrial products, and even fuels (one of the problems of Iran is that the Iranian ports do not have enough capacity to unload the items imported from other countries in a timely manner and it has to pay demurrage to many ship owners), destructed by 8 years of war (with Iraq), and headed by a bunch of Mullahs, can dare to stand in front of the important states of the world?

The answer to all of these questions is that the Islamic regime's officials are preparing this country to act as a suicide bomber.

They do not care what is going to happen to the country. No measure of threat, no extent of danger, no prospect of destruction and annihilation of the people, country and everything in between is important for the suicide bomber. The suicide bomber has no belongings and is not afraid of anything. He is going to sacrifice himself for the cause and nothing is going to stop him.

According to the Islamic ideology of the regime there is no unit in the world as country and the managers of the Islamic regime are not under any duty to protect the national interests of any country. They only recognize a unit called "Ummat" that includes the Islamic peoples. The area out of the land of the Muslims, according to what can be called the Islamic international law, is the territory of war (Darol-harb as opposed to Darol-Islam).

The Muslims live in peace with the Darol-harb until such time that they get the power to overcome the "enemies" and take their territories. Meanwhile, if the un-Islamic peoples choose to remain in their old religions, they have to pay a special tax called "Jazieeh" to the Islamic government.

On the other side, the idea of martyrdom has always been at the center of the Islamic ideology of the regime in Iran. The great teacher of the Islamic Revolution, Dr. Ali Shariati (he was a demagogue of the worst kind. He believed his own gibberish), whose role in victory of the so-called Islamic revolution in Iran was much more important than Khomeini's and Mullahs of Iran, had said: "The martyr is the heart of history".

The regime of Iran wants to go ahead in this course until the war and destruction begins. They need this war. They love war and armed confrontation. Khomeini called Iran-Iraq war (1980-1988) a God given gift.

The Iranian regime is always glorifying the "Uprising of Hussein". The case of Hussein is in fact a "mass-suicide mission". According to the religious stories, 72 persons that were companions of Hussein were killed in war against thousands of heavily armed troops of Yazid (headed by Shemer, the Armored [Zeljoushan]). Hussein and his companions were well aware they were going to die in the unequal war and in hand of the other side and still Hussein refused to accept the terms of ending the hostilities, which was accepting the dominance of Yazid as the leader of the Muslims. Hussein claimed that he was the leader of Muslims.

The countries of the world, whether big or small, have a limited scope of maneuver. This scope may differ according to many elements (natural resources, military power, level of education, foreign exchange reserves, industrial growth, international prestige and so on). Understanding and acting in the scope of the limitations is the art of living among the countries of the world. Those who do not understand these limitations and act without due regard to them are going to suffer everything from minor damage to annihilation and destruction. History is full of names of the states that do not exist anymore due to the mistake or arrogance of the political leaders. There is no glory in pushing a country to death and destruction. The Islamic Republic of Iran deserves no respect from the people of Iran for moving the people and territory of Iran towards a suicide mission. When there is no country, how can we feel good about independence? Independence in a traditional sense is dead. All countries of the world need each other and Iranian people (unlike the Iranian regime) are ready and willing to play their role in this game, after the collapse of the Islamic regime.

THE NUCLEAR CASE OF
IRAN AND THE SURVIVAL
OF THE ISLAMIC REGIME

Many people have addressed the nuclear case of Iran from the wrong angle. This is the reason for failure in getting the reasonable conclusions and also the root of repeated negotiation failures. From IRI's perspective, the central point in the present nuclear case of Iran is the survival of the ruling regime.

The Mullahs who rule Iran, according to their religious ideology, do not care about anything else other than preservation of power. Anyone, inside or outside of Iran, who looks at the present nuclear case of Iran, from any other angle than preservation of the regime, reaches the wrong calculations and faces contradictions.

The fact that Iran needs nuclear energy (due to the growing domestic oil consumption, dependence on oil exports, the low price of nuclear energy, the need to use oil in other ways as a national capital and many other reasons) has nothing to do with the efforts of the present regime of Iran for continuing its nuclear program. Providing "electricity" is not so important for the regime of Iran to risk its existence. The only aim of the nuclear program of Iran is to gain a guarantee against internal insurgency and possible intervention of foreign forces for changing the regime.

The regime is ready to use all kinds of forces to remain on top. The internal resistance in Iran is so brutally suppressed that even the reformists (the most lukewarm form of the forces that follow the change in the framework of the "Velayate Faghih"- the government of Mullahs), are fully neutralized. Undoubtedly, after the Presidential elections in Iran when the conservatives got rid of Khatami, the regime started a new wave of suppression and made sure that all of the resistance forces, including the reformists who have exposed themselves are out of the scene. The clear signs of this policy are already visible, but compared to what will be imposed after the next Presidential elections these are nothing. The situation after the next election will be like a creeping move by the conservative side of the Islamic Revolutionary Guards Corps which would give IRGC more positions of power. Therefore, the people of Iran, inside and outside of the country, are desperately looking for a savior. The regime of the Mullahs is well aware of this option and its main policy in front of that option is the nuclear program.

The fact that a number of conservatives and reformists (who are both followers of the Velayate Faghih) and also a number of the people from all political spectrums (even the dissidents) support the nuclear program of Iran is meaningless because the ruling circles in Iran do not care about what the people think of their polices. The apparent unity among the various factions and the people in support of the nuclear program is based on their wrong perceptions and mistaken beliefs, not common interests and clear understanding.

The Conservatives (led by Hayate Motalefeh, which has disguised itself as a party recently) are the ruling power and they want to remain in power and therefore they want the nuclear power (not electricity) to back them up. The Reformists (who follow the Velayate Faghih) had never any real power in Iran. During the last several years that the Reformists pretended to have power (only because a few of the Reformists were given powerless positions or positions that could be neutralized by the Conservations), all of their plans were rejected and finally they were totally and en mass disqualified.

The humiliated and embarrassed Reformists are trying to buy some kind of prestige for themselves by supporting what looks like "a national plan". The problem is that the Reformists, as persons believing in Velayate Faghih are not entitled to support any "national plans". They are bound by the rules of the game to follow the instructions of the "Guardian" or the Supreme Leader.

Velayate Faghih means that the people are like "minors" who need a "Guardian " and the Guardian is the Supreme Leader who is the personification of all divine forces on Earth. The regime has proved that it does not have the capacity to get reformed from the inside and the Reformists who support Valyate Faghih are wasting their time and energy. It is not important for the ruling circles of Iran and the people of Iran what the Reformists think.

The ordinary people of Iran who support the nuclear programs and sometimes say: "Israel and India and Pakistan have nuclear power, why not Iran?" speak out of national pride and national sentiment. While national pride can be good for promoting certain programs and policies if used at the right time as a way to inspire the people, if it is misused, at the wrong time and by the wrong people with insincere motives, it can push the nation toward destruction.

The ordinary people who support the nuclear program of Iran at the present juncture ignore the real problems of their society. Are the people of Iran, especially those who claim we should have nuclear power, ready to tolerate the international sanctions? (The regime has no problem with sanctions.

They will bribe their way out by high oil prices and create lucrative black market deals administered by the Aghazadeh-ha, the relatives of the Mullahs. They have extensive experience in violating the sanctions through the dealings with the Iraqis in the era of Saddam.) The people of Iran are living under hardship.

In spite of the good oil income, the majority of the people live under the poverty line.

30% of the people are unemployed. The corrupt economic system is giving all economic advantages to a certain group that act as the lackeys of the regime. Are these people ready to go under more pressures and see their children die because they want the Mullahs to have nuclear bombs, or "electricity"? Are the people of Iran ready to go to war to have a few low-level nuclear bombs, put at the tip of several outdated North Korean missiles that are repainted and called Shahab 1, 2, 3, that they would never dare to use against any foreign state, but will be certainly used against the people inside Iran if the people threaten the government of "the divinely assigned Mullahs and the deputies of the hidden imam on Earth"?

There is another interesting group that supports the nuclear program of Iran. This group consists of some Iranians who live out of Iran. Even though they will not to be the target of any sanctions imposed on Iran and are not going to send their children to the war fronts to be used along with donkeys as the minesweepers, they are adamant that the Mullahs should go ahead with the nuclear programs. The attitude of this group is like throwing a huge party on someone else's dime.

The only reason the Islamic Republic of Iran is pursuing the nuclear programs is to guarantee its own survival. The regime is ready to use the nuclear power against its own people if necessary; and according to the Islamic instructions, this is fully permitted. The problem is that there is a regime in Iran which concerns great world powers. These powers are not ready to let this particular regime have nuclear teeth. Therefore, while this regime is in power, it is the wrong time to defend the idea of Iran having nuclear power.

Some people think that nuclear power will bring security for Iran. What if it is proved that such is not case?

The nuclear program of Iran is not focused on the security for the country or state. It is about the security of a regime that is convinced is going to get into serious conflict with the West, as the symbol of a certain way of life and thinking that stands in contrast to the ideology of the regime of Iran. Look at the following sentences.

They are not from the opponents of the regime, human rights organizations, or the Israeli press. These are the direct words of Hassan Abbasi, the Director of Center of External Security Analysis of the Revolutionary Guards Corps, talking in Tehran University (05/23/04):

"The leaders of the Islamic world should have the courage to declare: Islam and Western democracy are not compatible. Islam has nothing in common with the Universal Declaration of the Human Rights. Islam has nothing in common with the Western liberalism and this kind of freedom. Islam opposes these ideas... According to Nietzsche, the founding of a civil society leads to the death of God...the Koran has said: go to war...if it is possible to do something that the disbelievers feel fearful, then, this kind of terrorism is holy terrorism.... Look at my hands.

These are the hands that have created Hizbullah, Hamas and Islamic Jihad... You have 6000 nuclear warheads... those are our target. The guerrillas will destroy them.... We are working on recruiting the Mexicans and Argentineans for our cause... We will mobilize everyone who has a complaint against America...we have identified all of their weak points... and we will give those information to the combatant groups of the world." (http://khba-barnameh.gooya.com/nabavi/archives/real/abbasi-hassan.rm)

The proposals for negotiations that are concentrated on other issues except than the survival of the regime will get nowhere. At the same time, any formula that helps to guarantee the survival of the regime will be greatly welcomed by the regime of Iran. In fact this is the only issue that the Islamic Republic is interested to talk about. All other issues especially detailed and technical points of the nuclear program are aimed at keeping the people inside and outside of the country busy and disoriented.

The reason that the Mullahs are convinced that this is the way for guaranteeing their power is in the treatment by the West.

What has happened in the past years has endorsed the view of the regime that the nuclear power can help to guarantee the survival of the regime. A look at the US treatment of North Korea as compared to Saddam's Iraq is a very good example. North Korea has declared that it has nuclear warheads.

It is no secret that North Korea, along with the open and covert nuclear markets of Pakistan, headed by that state's chief of the Nuclear Energy Agency, were instrumental in exporting the nuclear know-how to the other countries, including Iran. Yet, the West is treating the regime of North Korea with much caution, while the miserable Saddam who did not have those weapons is dead.

There is no doubt that the demand of the Western states from Iran to stop its nuclear program is totally in contradiction to the NPT and the other norms and regulations of international law and it may even offend some people's notion of justice. No politician, anywhere in the world, including Iran, is legally required to establish justice at the international level.

All of the government officials, from the highest to the lowest echelons, in all countries are ordered and instructed to pursue the "national interests" and if they do anything other than that, they are set aside. The declared national interest of the dominant powers of the world is focused on the point that the nuclear program of Iran is not trustworthy and they are going to stop the program one way or another.

The Iranian people and the government, as usual, must find the limitations of maneuver and the best option under these conditions. If the regime of Iran does not care about the national interests, national security, and the welfare of people and it is only pursing the interests of the ruling circle, why should the others support the nuclear policy? The regime of Iran is preparing itself for a war and claims this to be out of bravery. But the reality is that war is a necessity for a fascist regime. It is one of the standard definitions of a fascist regime.

Iran is using the differences of the USA and the EU for killing time and getting closer to the nuclear bomb. The differences between the Western countries are very serious. The main question is: are the Americans and Europeans ready to give guarantees to the regime of Iran for survival? The response of the Europeans is different from the USA's. The US does not trust and does not need the Iranian regime and considers it as a source of terrorism and trouble.

Contradictions between the UN Convention on the Rights of Women and the Iranian Islamic Law

The Convention on the Elimination of All Forms of Discrimination Against Women (CEDAW) was adopted in 1979 in the United Nations General Assembly. It has a preamble, and 30 articles. In the preamble, the states who are parties to the convention agree that any kind of discrimination against women is against the principle of equality of human beings. The member countries are also committed, in articles 2 to 6, to take immediate action to ensure the political, social, economic and cultural rights of women. Articles 10 to 14 obligate the states to treat men and women equally in the areas of education, occupation, health, and economic and social opportunities. The convention has become effective as of 1981.

What does the Convention want from the member states?

According to the UN Division for the Advancement of Women (http://www.UN.org/daw): "The Convention on the Elimination of All Forms of Discrimination against Women (CEDAW)... is often described as an international bill of rights for women... It defines what constitutes discrimination against women and sets up an agenda for national action to end such discrimination. The Convention defines discrimination against women as '...any

45

distinction, exclusion or restriction made on the basis of sex which has the effect or purpose of impairing or nullifying the recognition, enjoyment or exercise by women, irrespective of their marital status, on a basis of equality of men and women, of human rights and fundamental freedoms in the political, economic, social, cultural, civil or any other field.' By accepting the Convention, States commit themselves to undertake a series of measures to end discrimination against women in all forms, including:

* To incorporate the principle of equality of men and women in their legal system,

* Abolish all discriminatory laws and adopt appropriate ones prohibiting discrimination against women,

* To establish tribunals and other public institutions to ensure the effective protection of women against discrimination,

* To ensure elimination of all acts of discrimination against women by persons, organizations or enterprises. The Convention provides the basis for realizing equality between women and men through ensuring women's equal access to, and equal opportunities in, political and public life -- including the right to vote and to stand for election -- as well as education, health and employment. State parties agree to take all appropriate measures, including legislation and temporary special measures, so that women can enjoy all their human rights and fundamental freedoms...Countries that have ratified or acceded to the Convention are legally bound to put its provisions into practice. They are also committed to submit national reports, at least every four years, on measures they have taken to comply with their treaty obligations."

The convention has been the subject of serious controversies in Iran and other Islamic Countries.

The Iranian reform-oriented Sixth parliament ratified a bill paving the way for adhesion of Iran to the convention and immediately the Council of Guardians which is the watchdog of conservatives in Iran and it is actually more powerful than the Parliament and President of Iran put together, has rejected its ratification and decided that certain articles of the Convention are contrary to the rules of Islam.

Are the Convention articles contrary to the rules of Islam?

Yes, they are. The points of contradiction are so clear that they do need much discussion. Let's look at a few of them:

1- According to the rules of Islam, women share of inheritance is half of men's. The origin of this discrimination is rooted in the laws of the Arab nomads which assumed men as head of household and women as properties.

2- The "blood money" for women is half of men's. Blood money refers to the money a person who kills or disfigures another must pay to the victim's family. Because women are deemed to be worth half as men, blood money for women is half of the amount designated by the Islamic government for a man. The issue gets more interesting when one considers that the blood money for a certain part of the male gender (genitals) is almost equal the amount for an entire female person. One could conclude that it'd be cheaper to kill a woman than damage a man's private part. The concept of blood money is an outdated notion which underscores the discrimination between men and women. In today's society, this concept is really humiliating both for men and the women.

3- The right of divorce is absolute for men but not for women. The Islamic courts have tried to pretend that this right is not absolute for men, but looking at actual cases one can see that there is clear contradiction between the Islamic law on marriage and divorce with human rights' views on marriage and divorce.

4- Women are not allowed to travel without direct permission of their husbands or male supervisors (in case of girls, divorcees, and so on, a male supervisor is designated to supervise the female. In many cases the supervisor may lack moral competency and the sole criteria for this designation is being male). Travel is defined as stepping outside the house.

5- Women's testimony in court is worth half of a man's. In other words two female witnesses are considered the equivalent of one male witness. This principle is strictly observed in Islamic courts and formal attestations.

6- Women are not allowed to be judges under any circumstances. Recently in some countries they have devised a plan to respond to critics of the discriminating judicial system. On the surface, they allow women to act as the judge and issue a preliminary order subject to approval by a clergy who later issues the real verdict. So in these cases, the woman acts more like an advisor than a judge.

7- Child custody is always given to men. (Like many other points, an attempt is made to justify the rule by portraying it as a blessing to women based on the rationale that by not having custody women would not have to bear the financial burden of raising the children). This notion is again based on the Arab nomad's rituals, according to which women were nothing more than housewives and as such had no source of income other than what was provided by husbands.

8- Women who are members of a religious minority (in particular those religions that are not considered People of the Book) especially suffer all of the above-noted practices because they are doubly discriminated against for both being women and members of a minority group.

9- According to Shiite Islam, men can have up to four wives and unlimited concubines (mixture of female slaves and third class wives) which is discriminatory unless women can also have up to four husbands and unlimited concubines.

10- According to the Islamic laws of all Islamic countries, women who marry foreigners lose their citizenship rights but this is not true in the case of men.

11- When a person changes his/her religion from Islam to anything else (Ertedad), men are immediately condemned to death, but women are imprisoned and beaten several times every day (five times at the time of daily prayer) until they give up the new religion and return to Islam. The underlying reason for the distinction is not to show advantage towards women, rather the differential treatment stems from viewing women as being too feeble-minded for the change in religion to be lasting whereas in the case of men, his decision to change his religion is deemed as absolute and too final for imprisonment to make a difference and death is considered the only solution for the crime of turning away from Islam.

12- There is clear discrimination in Islamic rules about clothing of men and women. According to the dominant interpretations of Islamic code of dress, women should cover all of their body except the front of the face, and hands from wrist to fingers. The rest of the woman's body is considered (Owrat) which is private and must be concealed in public. There are no such restrictions for men. Men are only called upon not to look passionately at women.

In all of the above cases, I can name the articles of the convention and also the Universal Declaration of Human Rights, one by one, to show how the Islamic rules contradict them.

Some in Iran have suggested using the "Arabic Formula" for adhesion to the convention. That means giving a reservation at the time of adhesion, which is like this: "We sign this document on the condition of non-contradiction with the tenets of Islam." This is what is called "religious fraud" (Koollahe Shar-ee). It means that you sign the document and you refrain from enforcing any part of it that you don't like under the pretext of contradiction with Islam. There two major obstacles for this interpretation. Article 18 of the convention, and several articles of 1969 UN Convention on the law of treaties (Vienna Convention) and the decision of the International Court Justice in 1951, all clearly say: reservations that are in contradiction to the aim and purpose of a treaty are not acceptable. The reason that Arab countries have not faced serious objection for their practice is more political than legal and that is changing rapidly. Already there are numerous moves at the international level to discard this kind of reservation, especially in the case of humanitarian laws and regulations.

Some people, under different names, like religious intellectuals or reformists, have been trying to deny these contradictions and try to find ways to reconcile them with Islam. These spin doctors want people to believe that there is no contradiction between Islam and the UN convention. Here is what I think about these people:

1- They are not sincere. They want to reap benefits from both sides. In this sense, they are hypocrites. On the other hand, the opponents of the Convention, who are the conservative and fundamentalist, seem to be the more sincere and authentic followers of Islam, like the theological centers for Islamic women.

2- They deceive themselves and other people. They try to convince people about a form of religion that does not exist. A good example is all those who call themselves religious intellectuals. Intellectual cannot be religious. They are intellectuals who are boxed in by their own thinking. They have lost their way in their pursuit of truth and they are not brave enough to admit it. This is a serious case of arrogance. All of the so-called "scientific researches" who work for them are worthless. Their researches are based on pre-determined outcomes. Their findings precede the research. Their work does not measure up to the most basic scientific research criteria.

3- They waste people's time and energy. It seems that talking in vague terms has turned into an art in Iranian culture of writing. It is understandable how this custom could have been created as a result of living under corrupt and despotic regimes for a long period of time. But, it is time to set aside this custom and speak the truth plainly.

The solution is separating religion from politics, not pretending to invent a religion that does not exist. There is no religious solution for these cases.

WHAT IRANIAN WOMEN THINK ABOUT THE REGIME OF THE ISLAMIC REPUBLIC OF IRAN?

The Mullahs of Iran have wanted and still want to treat Iranian women as the Taliban did in Afghanistan. The only thing that did not let the regime do so was the determination and resistance of the Iranian society, especially the women, against the regime and its policies. Mistreating women in Iran comes from the inherent features of the Mullahs, as people engaged in the profession of demagogy. The Mullahs are under strict obligations according to the teachings of the nomadic Arabs of 1400 years ago to treat women as such.

There are many controversies about the approach of Islam to many issues. There are countless interpretations of main source texts on every subject that are not always in agreement; however, when it comes to the station of women in society, all the sources agree slavery of women. Starting from Koran, you can see numerous clear indications that women are considered as property.

The Mullahs of Iran have been trying seriously to change the approach of the Iranian society, especially women, on women's issues. In fact, the only sign indicating Iran observes Islamic laws as the regime claims is with respect to the regime's treatment of women. However, despite their best effort to enslave women, in the following examples they have failed to persuade the society at large:

1- To reduce to the extent they desired the social status of the Iranian women

2- To convince women as a group to strictly follow the religious rules against their rights and interests

3- To make woman of Iran a group that blindly supports the regime and tolerates social abuse and statutory mistreatment as an acceptable approach

4- To turn Iranian women into a group who is socially inactive, disillusioned and disappointed who mainly sits at home and concentrates on raising kids

Today, after 30 years of oppression, violation of human rights, tyrannical mistreatment and so on, the Iranian women are:

1- As free minded as they have always been in the history of this country

2- More aware of their rights

3- More ready to act for getting their rights

4- In the forefront of war against the Mullah's tyranny

5- The great admirers of secularism

    1- A great force calling for change in the line of equality, democracy and freedom in Iran.

IRANIAN WOMEN
AGAINST WOMEN'S RIGHTS

Couple of years ago I was attending a meeting in the Center for Post-Graduate Studies in International affairs of the Tehran University and I came to know through the officials of the center that they have been training a group of the Iranian women in order to take part in the international forums and represent the women of Iran.

Later I understood that these women were in fact a bunch of Islamic zealots imposed upon the same center for a training course and in fact their mission was sabotaging the women's rights in the international forums according to the Islamic ideology of the nomadic Arabs of the ancient Arabia.

These kinds of women are an embarrassment for the whole society of Iran. A country that had female kings in its history is now so miserable, under the Islamic-Arabic regime that a group of women are trying to stop the development of the women's rights. These women are a new kind of representatives popped up in the Islamic Republic of Iran. These representatives are supposed to act against the rights of the groups that they represent.

Let us take the case of the women who represent the women of Iran in the Majles and the officials that are supposed to defend the rights of women in the level of the governmental organizations. Usually when the parliament of Iran discusses an issue related to the women's rights (such as the adhesion of Iran to the UN documents for eradication of discrimination against women) more than any other group, these women who are "planted" in the Majles as the representatives of the people are in the fore-front of acting against adoption of any positive action. These women act as the Islamic robots controlled by the Mullahs and they usually utter the most disgusting and humiliating positions against the women of Iran.

The men and women of Iran are equally embarrassed to have such "diluted" elements among them who enjoy acting as the par-liamentarian prostitutes. As compared to the street prostitutes who sell their body out of misery and poverty, and they deserve all kinds of respect, these parliamentarian prostitutes do not deserve any respect.

Anytime that one of them opens her filthy mouth and speak against the women's rights, the whole people of Iran feel sad and embarrassed. Look at this piece of news that I have translated from a Persian website into English:.... "the spokesperson for the Women's Society of [Iranian] Islamic Revolution has told the correspondent of the political service of ISNA [Iranian Students News Agency] in Tehran: as far as the issue of the presence of women in the meetings of the Majles-e Khobreghan [someho the equivalent of the Constitutive Assembly in the Islamic-Ara-bic regime of Iran] is concerned, notthat nothing has changed in the laws of the elections of the Majles-e Khobreghan, the Soci-ety which follows the line of the fundamentalist forces, will act according to the principles. Masoumeh Hamidzadeh told ISNA: they make much ado before each election, but at the moment we [Women's Society of Islamic Revolution] see no need for par-ticipation and presence of women in the Majles-e Khobreghan because the presence of the men is enough." Also, I remember that several years ago (I think 2000), the Iranian delegation of women in the International Congress of Women (one of the greatest occasions in the history of the women's rights that was attended by several thousand women representing govern-ments and international organizations and the NGOs) were try-ing to stop the congress from adopting resolutions in the line of women's rights. They were acting apparently under the pretext of the cultural differences of various areas of the world, but the real concern of the Iranian female delegation was defending the instructions of the Islamic-Arabic regime of Iran based on the barbaric and nomadic Arab laws. The Iranian women have suffered from the double-discrimination under the Islamic regime of Iran. They have been under the same restrictions as men in an undemocratic and anti-human rights regime of the Islamic Republic and at the same time they have suffered more discrimination for being woman.

These women are a new kind of representatives popped up in the Islamic Republic of Iran. These representatives are supposed to act against the rights of the groups that they represent. Let us take the case of the women who represent the women of Iran in the Majles and the officials that are supposed to defend the rights of women in the level of the governmental organizations.

Usually when the parliament of Iran discusses an issue related to the women's rights (such as the adhesion of Iran to the UN documents for eradication of discrimination against women) more than any other group, these women who are "planted" in the Majles as the representatives of the people are in the forefront of acting against adoption of any positive action. These women act as the Islamic robots controlled by the Mullahs and they usually utter the most disgusting and humiliating positions against the women of Iran.

The men and women of Iran are equally embarrassed to have such "diluted" elements among them who enjoy acting as the parliamentarian prostitutes. As compared to the street prostitutes who sell their body out of misery and poverty, and they deserve all kinds of respect, these parliamentarian prostitutes do not deserve any respect. Anytime that one of them opens her filthy mouth and speak against the women's rights, the whole people of Iran feel sad and embarrassed. Look at this piece of news that I have translated from a Persian website into English:.... "the spokesperson for the Women's Society of [Iranian] Islamic Revolution has told the correspondent of the political service of ISNA [Iranian Students News Agency] in Tehran: as far as the issue of the presence of women in the meetings of the Majles-e Khobreghan [somehow Many of the crimes against women in the Islamic regime of Iran are not reported. You know why? Because: they are against the "religious based" honor of the family and the society. I do not think the word "honor" can be more degraded, humiliated and mortified in any other way.

The men and women, inside and outside of the disgusting regime of Iran, who close their eyes to the heinous crimes against women under the pretext of honor, are most dishonorable creatures of the world. The Islamic regime of Iran is not ready to accept and implement the United Nations Convention on Eradication of all kinds of Discrimination against Women (in a nutshell, the convention says that men and women are equal) because the barbaric laws of the nomadic ancient Arabs is not prepared for such a rudimentary principle. I do not know how the women who do not believe in the equality of men and women can defend the rights of women?

The problem is not that Iranian women do not like to be free and respected. The problem is not that Iranian men do not care about the rights of their mothers, daughters, sisters, spouses and so on. The problem lies in the Islamic regime of Iran and it will be solved when the regime is returned to the dustbin of the history.

ISRAELIS AND IRANIANS
ARE NATURAL ALLIES

The regime of Iran pretends that there is a deep hostility between Iranians and Israel. On the other side, the regime of Iran has been trying to prove that the Iranian people care about Palestinians in a special way (let say different from their feeling about the Chechens in Russia). Both of these claims are baseless and wrong. Iranians do not feel any hostility towards Israelis and Iranians have no special place in their hearts for the Arab Palestinians. Iranians had a great role in the ancient history of the Jews.

The name of Cyrus the great is mentioned many times in the Old Testament. Cyrus freed the Jews while they were living in exile and under captivity in Babylon. He let them return to Jerusalem and helped them to build their main temple. The dates of these events are occasions for some of the most important celebrations of the Jews. This is also a source of great honor for Iranians as the flag bearers of the religious tolerance, human rights, and respect for the "others".

In addition to these historical relations, there are many seminaries between Iran and Israel, such as:

1- Iran, like Israel, is a non-Arab country in the Middle East. Amir Taheri, a prominent Iranian journalist, has mentioned in his recent article (dated March 24, 2006): "If Israel had never appeared on the map, the energy of the pan-Arab nationalism movement, which dominated Arab politics in the post-war era, would have been directed against two other neighbors: Turkey and Iran. To a certain extent, it was anyway. Even today, the Arab League claims that the Turkish province of Iskanderun is 'usurped Arab territory' and regards the Iranian province of Khuzestan as 'occupied Arab land'."

2- Iran and Israel both follow a religion that is different from the Arabs. Israelis are mostly Jews, and Iranians are mostly Shiite (Sunni do not consider Shiites as a branch of Islam in many Arab countries). Iranians are not serious Muslims (compare the behaviors of Iranians to the people of the Arab countries) and it is accepted by some researchers that Shiite sect was "invented" by Iranians as a kind of instrument to be different from the Sunni Arabs.

3- Iran, like Israel, is accused by the Arabs for being an occupier of the Arab lands. The case of Israel is clear and the case of Iran is related to the three Islands in the Persian Gulf that the UAE has put a claim on them. (The UAE did not exist before 1971).

Therefore, the two countries must have the best relations. However, the government of the Islamic Republic of Iran claims to be the first enemy of Israel. Why? Because: the government of the Islamic Republic is also the worst enemy of the Iranian people. A look at the record of the Islamic Republic of Iran reveals that that during the last quarter of the century, this regime has done everything possible to eradicate the Iranian identity of Iran. If they have not succeeded to do so, it was not due to their failure to work hard or their use of less violent tactics as compared to the Afghan Talibans. The reason was that the people of Iran did not let them to get what they wanted. The regime of Iran is determined to use the case of Israel as:

1- a pretext to fight the people of Iran who do not feel any hostility towards the Israelis.

2- The regime has failed in all cultural, economic, and political fields and it wants to find an enemy to accuse for its failures. 3- The regime of Iran has lost its legitimacy and it is trying to find a mission for itself. The people of Iran do not feel to have a special obligation to defend the rights of the Palestinians too. There are countless Arab countries, with money and power and good relations and they are in much better position to defend the Palestinians. In fact, the Arabs, including the Palestinians, never have asked or welcomed the intervention of the Iranian regime in the Palestinian issue. They consider this as Arabic issue and consider the intervention of Iran as step from the "outside" and they look at Iran as they look at Israel. During the Iran-Iraq war (1980-1988), no Arab country or person, including the Palestinians and the Syrians, who were fed by the Iranian regime, participated on behalf of Iran. As far as the case of three Iranian Islands in the Persian Gulf is concerned, all Arab states, including Palestinians and Syrians, have stood behind the baseless claims of the UAE. Perhaps one of the most important acts during the Iraq-Iran war (1980-1988) was the daring attack of Israel against the nuclear facilities of Iraq (Osiraq). If Saddam had managed to complete its nuclear bomb, he would not have hesitated one second for using it against Iran (Khomeini was the same).

When the new president of Iran, who is under education for learning the Alphabet of politics, claimed that Israel should be wiped out or the Holocaust did not exist, the people of Iran showed no sympathy. However, many Arabs, who do not dare to speak out for themselves, got happy. Some people in Iran showed their disagreement with the president by asking: "whose president are you? Iranians or Palestinians?" Are we out of problems that we want to solve the problems of the other countries?

THE BATTLE OF ALCOHOL AND
NARCOTIC DRUGS IN IRAN

According to Islam, as interpreted by the Islamic regime of Iran, consumption of Alcoholic beverages is completely prohibited and it is considered a sin. On the basis of the same religious ideology the Islamic regime of Iran has legislated criminals codes, which envisage punishments for those who produce, consume and deal with alcoholic beverages of any kinds. The same laws say that if a person is arrested three times for consumption of alcoholic beverages (no degree of alcohol in blood or any other criterion that refers to being in the state of "drunkenness" is not mentioned in the laws and the disciplinary forces can arrest anyone that they suspect of having consumed alcoholic beverages, and usually their criteria is the smell of alcohol coming out of the mouth of the suspects, can be arrested) can be condemned to "execution".

Therefore, a person that has consumed several beers and he or she is arrested for the thirds time, he or she can face death penalty. The first and second times lead to prison terms, lashes and Islamic torture called "Ta'azir". Usually the sentences are handed over by the "revolutionary courts. The courts that look into such matters are called "Social Vices Courts". They are apparently independent but organizationally they are a part of the revolutionary court and the judges of these courts are appointed through the officials of the Islamic Revolutionary Courts and they make their judgments with the same laws and regulations as the revolutionary courts.

In other words these courts act illegally and do not observe any law except than what is written in the books of the religious rulings of the big Ayatollahs, especially so- called Imam Khomeini. However, these books of rulings of the big Ayatollahs are almost the same, as if they have copied from each other. (The reality is that the big ones have all copied from the same sources: the most important source is the books of Mohammad Bagher Majlesi, or Alameh Majlesi, who lived in Safavid period and he headed the Mullahs of that time).

On the other side, there is no single ruling in the Islamic regime of Iran, even by the second and third class Mullahs (let alone the big cats) that forbid narcotic drugs. In fact, the Mullahs have long been the loyal customers of narcotic drugs. There is not any reference to the narcotic drugs in the books of rulings of the Ayatollahs (a great part of these "books of Rulings" or Ressalahs are devoted to the rituals of prayers for women in the different stages of their monthly period. The description of these rituals is mentioned so meticulous and sometimes with pornographic details in all Rassalahs of the Grand Ayatollahs. These details are related to the ancient Arabic nomads thinking that considered women in the monthly period as "morally" dirty). However, there is no single thing about the narcotic drugs I the books of rulings or Fatwas of the Ayatollahs.

The Organizations in charge of campaign against narcotic drugs in Iran have been frustrated by failing to find a religious ruling against narcotic drugs (while everything is administered in the Islamic regime of Iran by the same sources). Out of desperation, they have adopted a sentence from Khomeini for doping their job and that sentence says: "one is not allowed to do harm to himself." This sentence is of course taken out of context by those miserable officials who were trying to find a religious basis for their job. In fact, Khomeini has never meant to say this sentence about prohibition of the narcotic drugs.

The end line is that many of the young Iranians who may have answered their quest for some kind of refreshment by drinking couple of beers, have resorted to using various kinds of the narcotic drugs. After all it is less risky for them to use drugs than alcoholic beverages of any kind.

Iran is basically a transit route for the international trade of the narcotic drugs. Although the role of Iran as the transit route has not changed during the last decades, the rest of the route has gone under considerable developments. The" Golden Triangle" is not using the old routes. Instead, the mafia of narcotics that is dependent on the products in Afghanistan, and Pakistan, flow their products through Iran to the European countries (very little to the USA and North America. The latter is almost completely fed by the Latin American sources).

The semi-official route of the drug traders is: Afghanistan-Iran-Caspian Sea-EU. (Formerly it was Golden Triangle-Iran-Turkey-Eastern Europe-EU.). The fact that Iran has stayed there as the main transit route has contributed to the expansion of consuming narcotic in Iran. The policy of the Islamic regime in suppressing Alcoholic beverages (a religious sin and a violation of the criminal code) and at the same time, refraining from prohibition of the narcotic drugs has resulted in a disaster in Iran. Iran has one of the highest numbers of drug addicts in the world. More than half of the prisoners in the 200,000 populations of the Iranian prisons are drug users and dealers.

You can add the following reasons to those mentioned above for this disaster:

1- Lack of enough social disdain towards the narcotic drugs.

2- Introduction of new kinds of narcotics drugs, including the "psychotropic substances" (downers and uppers) to the market of Iran

3- Cheap and easy availability of the narcotic drugs and psychotropic substances in the market. Sometimes they cheaper than ordinary cigarettes.

4- The huge number of the young people in the population that are deprived from many kinds of recreational facilities

5- The massive number of the unemployed persons in the society

6- The local cultures of addiction in some parts of the country

7- The business of narcotic drugs in a systematic way in some parts, especially the southeast and northeast of Iran.

8- The growing sophistication of the traders of the narcotic drugs. Some gangs in the south of Iran are equipped with anti-aircraft rockets, and heavy guns.

9- The growing relations of the traders in narcotic drugs, as organized criminal institutions, sometimes called "narco-terrorists" with the terrorist organizations.

10- Lack of the control by the police and military forces, especially in the border areas.

11- The extensive corruption of the police and military forces dealing with the narcotic drug dealers. This issue results in returning of a lot of discovered narcotic drugs back to the circulation of the market.

12- Consumption of narcotic drugs among the Iranian educated persons is mind blowing. You can hardly find a physician of any kind or an engineer in Iran that do not use narcotic drugs. They only use more expensive types of drugs or pay more for the same level of the narcotics. Consuming narcotic drugs has turned into the main type of recreation for many Iranian professional and educated people in Iran. I am sure the sense of being frustrated in the Islamic regime of Iran has a great role to play in pushing these types of the Iranians towards the narcotic drugs.

The Islamic regime of Iran is responsible for a major part of the expansion of the addiction to narcotic drugs in Iran and the next regime of Iran will have to tackle with this problem soon after the collapse of the Mullahs dictatorship.

IRAN AND PALESTINE

The remarks of Supreme Leader Khamenie and President Ahmadinejad, make it look like Iran is a country which is deeply interested and cares about the issue of Palestine and Israel. The reality is that most of the Iranians do not know where Palestine is and almost all of Iranians do not care what has happened to the Palestinians. Then, how come the leaders of the Islamic Republic of Iran, starting from Khomeini and up to the current president, keep talking about the issue of Palestine as if it is Iran's first priority? It is very clear. It is not possible to attend to Iran's problems through inefficient and demagogue managers but it is easy to talk about the Palestinians.

After more than 30 years of Islamic propaganda to include holding ceremonies on certain days for commemoration of the Palestinian issues, paying billions of dollars to the Palestinians, selling cheap and even giving free oil to the crooked Syrian government officials for supporting the Hezbollah and Hamas, after building thousands of meaningless statues, and other things for Ghods (the Dome of Rock) and naming the streets of Iran with religious Arabic names, and bringing the Palestinians to Iran for hospitalization, paying rewards to the suicide killers and other acts, the Iranians are no closer to the Palestinians. Some Iranians might have had sympathy for Palestinians in the past, but as explained below that's also gone.

Iranians have no interest in the fate of Palestine as long as their own fate is under question through the irresponsible and illogical acts of the leaders of the Islamic Republic of Iran. Iranians do not want to spend even 1 cent to support the cause or well-being of the Palestinians as long as a third of the Iranian population lives under the poverty line in Iran. The Iranians do not care what happens to the Palestinians as long as Iranian rights are not respected and recognized by any Arab country. The Arabs have always threatened Iran. Among the Iranian neighbors, Iraq always had problems with Iran. Iran and Iraq were on the verge of fighting at the time of Shah. The only thing that stopped the Iraqis was the powerful army of Iran.

During the last several months that the new president of the Islamic Republic of Iran was put in the post of presidency by the circles of power and through rigged elections, he has spoken more about the issues related to Palestine than Iran. Some people have even asked "Is he president of Palestine or Iran?" Iran's delusional president has started to rehash some of the old issues about Palestine as if he has invented the topic. As far as the Iranians' consideration of Palestine, below are the most important points:

1- The Palestinians are no more important than the Russian Chechens and other Muslims for the people of Iran.

2- Iranians are not serious Muslims.

3- Iranians are Shiite which is different than the religion of Palestinians and other Arabs

4- Palestinian issue is not a Muslim question. It is an Arab issue. The other countries are using the issue as an excuse to impose certain political ideas.

5- Iranians, according to their national interests, must be the closest ally of Israel

6- The Arab countries already regard Iran as an ally of Israel. The Arabs do not like the "meddling" of the Islamic Republic in the Arab issue of Palestine and they feel humiliated that Iran talks about the issue more the Arabs.

7- Many Arabs have long looked at Iranians as "Majoos" [Zoroastrian], Ajam [Non-Arab], and Rafezi [one who has created a religion other than what Islam has instructed and therefore, Rafezi stands for meanings like traitors and unbelievers]. The Arab countries think that Iran like Israel is an occupier of the Arab Lands, referring to the three Iranian Islands that were returned to Iran by the British after their withdrawal from the East of Suez. Iran was instrumental in independence of the UAE, and out of regular disrespect, the Arabs of the UAE are now claiming that the Iranian Islands belong to them. When Iran took back its islands (and failed to get back some others like Bahrain], the UAE did not exist as a legal entity.

8- During the Iran-Iraq war (1980-1988), due to their hostility to Iran, the Arabs provided Iraq with all kinds of financial assistance, military support and even sent troops there to fight as mercenaries (the issue of Saddam and the war crimes of Iraq will be covered in a separate piece later). Not even one Palestinian has ever supported the rights of Iran.

9- Iranians have only suffered from the issue of Palestine because some of the Iranian terrorists that took part in toppling the regime of Shah in Iran were trained in the Palestinian resistance groups.

Opposition and
the Regime of Iran

The regime of the Islamic Republic of Iran has managed to stay in power for the last quarter of century, in spite of its inefficiency and corruption. The regime has lasted for 30 years but one never knows if it'll be in power tomorrow. Even the allies of this regime do not understand how such a corrupt and illogical regime has lasted. It is not baseless that some people in Iran think that the "Hidden Imam" (supernatural forces) is protecting the regime, because they can find no other explanation for survival of this regime.

There are various reasons for this survival, but undoubtedly one of the most important reasons is the lack of a viable opposition. Most of the forces that call themselves opposition are not real opposition. They pretend to be opposition. In fact, the opposition that does not believe in the collapse of the regime of the Islamic Republic of Iran is not opposition at all. The forces inside and outside Iran that they think they can change the political structure of Iran without casting aside the doctrine of Velayate-Faghih [Dominance of the Mullah's government], are wasting their time and deceiving the people of Iran.

Real opposition must prove that it is an alternative to the existing regime. In other words, if the opposition is going to work under the same doctrine as the existing regime, then we are only talking of taking out some figures and putting some others in their place. This change means nothing but personal gains for the self-proclaimed opposition leaders.

For example, if the existing regime violates human rights, through degradation of women, depriving people from basic freedoms of expression, assembly, speech, religion and so on, the opposition, if it is real and not in name only, must prove that it stands for the opposite of the existing regime's practices meaning that it believes women have the freedom to choose how they dress and no dress code is imposed on them by the government, people are free to choose their religion, the press is free and so on.

If the present regime of Iran believes in staging false elections, establishing sham parliament, and selecting a few persons as supreme figures when they lack social responsibility, accountability and transparency, and at the same time the same irresponsible figures are the ones who hold the real control of all political and economic forces in the country, the opposition must show that they are on the other side of the spectrum and they believe in free elections, democracy and transparency. Velayate-Faghih, as the exiting doctrine of government in Iran does not believe in any of these. Therefore, it is not possible to seek an alternative to the present regime, without casting out its dominant doctrine.

If Velayate-Faghih is the only form of government that Islam has to offer, then Islam is not able to be the basis on which modern society is built. What is the social, political, economic, and cultural plan of the Velayate Faghih? If what has happened in Iran in the last quarter of century is an example of this doctrine, then other than dominance of a group of Islamic clergymen, Velayate Faghih has nothing to offer.

The doctrine that claims to be the basis for the Iranian government is a "creature" fabricated by a group of Mullahs without any religious grounds. They have taken a self-styled interpretation from some of dubious religious sources to say that in the absence of the government by the Hidden Imam (the 12th Imam according to the "Ithna-ashari" or 12 Imams version of Shiite, which is dominant version of Shiite in Iran) the "deputies of the Hidden Imam", who are the big Ayatollahs, would form the government.

Those who are ready to accept this gibberish, as the basis of a new government cannot be an alternative to the present regime. At the same time, those who are not ready to offer political and economic plans other than the programs of the existing regime, have no chance of getting the position of a serious opposition to eventually replace the regime. No force in or out of Iran can be regarded as real opposition if they do not oppose the Velayate Faghih. Those who do not oppose Velayate Faghi represent people who seek nothing other than personal preferences in the framework of the government of Mullahs. Therefore, the starting point for formation of the opposition and the first step toward unification of the opposition must be rejection of the Velayate Faghih.

POLITICIANS OF THE ISLAMIC REPUBLIC OF IRAN: TRAINING ON THE JOB

The people of Iran have always demonstrated a great capacity for transforming the extremists, hardliners, despots and politically naïve figures into moderate, civilized and even conservative persons. During the long history of Iran, the people of this land have succeeded to absorb and transform the invaders like Alexander the Great, the nomadic Arabs and the barbaric Mongols into civilized persons. However, this transformation process of turning the uncivilized and inexperienced into the civil and seasoned politician is not limited to dealing with foreign invaders and many of the domestic politicians also go through this process in Iran.

Alexander the Great was so fascinated by the Iranian culture and civilization that he accepted many governmental arrangements of Iran. The nomadic Arabs that invaded Iran under the banner of Islam were so incorporated into the government and political system of Iran that gradually they were left with nothing from their Arabic origins except than a few Arabic words with Persian accent. Iranian even wrote the grammar of Arabic language for the illiterate Arabs. Many features of Iran's rich culture can be seen in the architecture, fine arts, literature, and philosophy of Arab, as well as other, countries.

The Mongols were among the most barbaric and inhumane races in the world. When they first invaded Iran, in some cities after killing the whole population they killed cats and dogs so that they make everything Iranian disappear. However, it look several decades for Mongols to become such devout Iranians and even becoming Muslims that they took many new steps to spread the Iranian culture. One of the Mongol kings (Oljaito, the grandson of Mongol Emperor who named himself Sultan Mohammad Khodabandeh after converting to Islam) came up with a brilliant idea that if he had the time to implement it, many of the present day calculations would have been changed in the region.

He ordered the construction of the Sultanieh Dome (the biggest dome in Iran, and one of the greatest historical buildings in the world situated in Sultanieh near Zanjan of Iran) and he planned to transfer the tombs of all prominent Imams there. Also, the Mongols ruled as the biggest kings of the Indian sub-continent after learning governance in Iran. Almost all big historical monuments of India (including Taj Mahal in Agra) belong to the Mongols' era.

These characteristics of Iran are not limited to the foreigners, invaders and aliens. In modern history also, Iran has managed to train many of the domestic politicians. Only in the last 30 years, and during the time that some people call the second invasion of Iran by the Arabs, an army of illiterate Mullahs (which is an oxymoron because Mullah means learned) and their lackeys have been trained in Iran. The on-the-job training has included almost all ministers of the government, the members of the parliament, the ruling gang of the Leader's office, the generals of the revolutionary army, the judges of the revolutionary courts, managers of the state organizations and so on.

Khomieni was the biggest trainee in the Iranian government and politics. It took more than 8 years, killing and injuring of over two million people in Iran and Iraq, and thousands of POWs, MIAs and chemically injured people for him to know that whatever the self-proclaimed generals of the Revolutionary Guards were telling him about capturing Karbala in Iraq was based on ignorance about international politics. He likened accepting peace with Iraqı to drinking "the chalice of poison" and shortly after the war ended, he died.

Just look at the so-called "Students Following the Line of Imam". They were a number of self-proclaimed students (many of them did not even know where the university was) that attacked the American Embassy (for the second time!) in Tehran and took the personnel of the embassy as hostage for 444 days and illegally confiscated the embassy documents. Khomeini wanted to arrest them first but later he came to know that the students have found interesting materials about the relations of many of his close allies with the Americans.

He supported the embassy takeover and called this event a "Second Revolution that was even bigger than the first one!" A great number of these so-called students were assigned later to important governmental posts. For instance, Sheihkolislami became the deputy foreign minister for a long time, Mirdamadi became the Chairman of the Parliamentary Committees, most of the others gained important jobs in the ministry of foreign affairs and the intelligence agencies of Iran and a number of them who belonged to the communist party or the MKOs (Mujahedine Khalgh who at that time, were Islamic Marxists. At the moment no one, not even the MKOs, know what they are) were arrested and executed later.

How strange that the leaders of the invading students are now among the reformists in Iran! Many of the so-called students after their "graduation" from the school of political midgets like Abbas Abdi have joined the moderate forces and they now support reforms. The mullah who apparently managed the so-called students (Mousavi Khoeiniha) has become so moderate that he has serious problems with the extremist elements in the Islamic Republic! The interpreter of the gang was a minister in the cabinet of the so-called reformist Khatami (Masoumeh Ebtekar, known as Mary).

Most of the prominent "students in the line of Imam" admit that they would not have participated in the American Embassy takeover if they could turn back the clock. It is interesting that when it was said the president-elect of Iran was a member of the student gang who attacked the American Embassy, the Iranian Islamic government made propaganda that he was not a party to this shameful act. They had forgotten that this was an honor for them!

The ruling trainees in the Islamic Republic, with different but often low IQ, hardly believed that what they have established is only a corrupt structure with a tint of religion. Nobody could convince people like Gholam Hussein Karbaschi (the former Mayor of Tehran), and Attaollah Mohajerani, the former Deputy of the President in Legal and Parliamentary Affairs and also the Minister of Culture and Islamic Guidance, that the Revolutionary Courts were Kangaroo courts that condemn people to sentences without due process.

The judges of the Revolutionary Courts were illiterate Mullahs that did not observe even the outdated Islamic codes. However, when these people themselves were faced with the judicial apparatus which they themselves had helped to establish, they understood the depth of their ignorance. The former Representative of Iran to the United Nations (Rejaie Khorasani) did not take part in any occasion regarding the United Nations. Asked about the reason he had said: "I am not a man of the UN Charter". It is interesting that after the long tenure of his representation in the United Nations he recommended that Iran quit the United Nations Organization!

INTERESTING BUSINESSES IN THE ISLAMIC REPUBLIC OF IRAN

The Islamic Republic of Iran is the home to some of the strangest professions and businesses in the world. These professions and businesses have religious and political dimensions. Here are some of them.

Bagpipe prayers

In the so-called holy cities of Qom and Mashhad, there are people who make money by charging for "reciting prayers in a bagpipe". This is how it works: these people have supposedly recited certain prayers previously and literally blew air into a bagpipe which is supposed to physically contain the breath of the person who recites the prayers. These people go around the shrines and similar places (especially the mosques attached to the shrines) and if paid certain amount of money, which is negotiable based on a price list (the longer prayers would cost more), they open the bagpipe and let the previously blown "prayer" out of the bagpipe in the presence of the customer. This way the customer gets his prayer and he does not have to waste him time standing around while the prayer is being recited.

Sex and the city

Another interesting profession is those whose job is to perform the special ritual for the temporary marriage. This is one of the rituals of the nomadic Arabs from "the time of Ignorance" (i.e.

before Islam) that has found its way to some Muslim societies. It is not necessary, according to the Islamic Shiite rules, that an expert or a clergyman perform the special code of the temporary marriage. (Sunnis claim that Islam does not allow temporary marriage. According to the Sunnis, it was only for several days during certain wars that the Prophet had given permission to the Muslims to have temporary marriage and eat donkey meat.

In contrast with permanent marriage which requires parental consent and witnesses, the temporary marriage does not require witnesses or any permission from anybody. In fact every person (that means every man) can recite the sentences in Arabic and get the "contract" concluded. The text of those sentences generally says "I enter into the temporary marriage contract with someone (a woman) for certain days or hours and in lieu of paying certain amount of money." The concerned woman has only to utter two words: "I agree" which is "ghabilto" in Arabic. However, since almost all of the Shiites of Iran do not understand and are not comfortable with using Arabic words (most of the Islamic religious minorities in Iran are Sunni), they usually need someone to perform the ritual. Here comes the new and lucrative profession of reciting the Arabic words for the contact of the temporary marriage. The interesting point is that the temporary marriage is only a "religious hat" for a kind of prostitution. The parties to the business of temporary marriage are usually the men who are looking for sex on the open market, the women who are paid for providing sexual services (including but not restricted to the normal prostitutes), and the performers of the ritual in Arabic. There is no limit for the number of times a man can have temporary marriage.

The defenders of the temporary marriage claim that this system gives a chance to the people who can't afford to get married (due to the high cost of permanent marriage), to have access to sexual services and avoid "illegal" and immoral activities. However, what has happened in practice is that the cost of temporary marriage is also high and usually the married and well-to-do men are the customers of this market. The Islamic regime of Iran has tried to use the temporary marriage as a safety valve for the masses of the young people (over fifty percent of the society), but the end result is adding a "legal channel" for the affluent layers of the society to commit adultery. Even the spouses of the Iranian Islamic officials and clergymen are seriously opposed to the temporary marriage because their husbands, as the men who have access to money and power, are at the forefront of the customers (solicitors) for the temporary marriage.

Transaction with God

Another interesting business in the Islamic regime of Iran is also related to prayers. According to the rulings of the experts in the Islamic jurisprudence (called Fughaha), which may or may not be a real interpretation of Islam, the people who have somehow neglected to perform their daily or other compulsory prayers (there are many kinds of middle level and arbitrary prayers too), can "buy" prayers from someone who undertakes to perform those prayers on their behalf. This is a great business with religious, financial and political dimensions.

Each person has the duty to perform five times (17 units) of daily prayers. So if you suppose that someone has not prayed for the last 30 years, the calculations on the basis of one dollar for every unit will be: 30 (years) multiplied by 365 days (with discount on leap years), multiplied by 17 (units). The result is: $ 151,200. There are special offices in the religious cities (and other cities) that get money from people based on the number of neglected prayers (if you like you can add some money for arbitrary prayers, like the midnight prayer, too) and they refer the "job" to "suitable" persons. These suitable persons are usually the good servants of the regime (religious students, clergymen and others). Most probably they get the money and after a while confirm that they have performed the task.

This business is not restricted to "prayers" per se. The scope of this lucrative market contains the "fasting period" (how many days the concerned person or some other person that he or she chooses has neglected to fast), negligence to go to Mecca while the concerned person was eligible to do so, payment of religious dues (in some cases includes one fifth of the entire property of a person), negligence in payment of the "imam's share". In addition to the "mandatory" prayers and religious duties, if the applicant so desires, they may also include "voluntary prayers and/or religious acts".

Correspondence with the Islamic Messiah

Jamkaran is a village near Qom in the South of Tehran. It is the home for the lucrative business of corresponding with the Imam e Zaman or the Hidden Imam or the Islamic Messiah. According to the Islamic-Shiite stories, Imam e Zaman will appear and enforce justice all over the world. The Shiites have been waiting for his appearance for the last 14 centuries. Again, according to the Islamic-Shiite stories, anyone who wants to send a letter to Imam e Zaman can write it and throw it in any flowing underground current or well.

However, the business-minded demagogues have made up stories that the water well in Jamkaran has a better chance of getting the messages to the Hidden Imam because some of the religious figures have seen things in their dreams (dreams and their interpretation are important phenomenon in the social and political history of the Islamic countries.

Recently, one of the Iranian Ayatollahs reported that he had seen the Hidden Imam in his sleep and he has approved the credentials of the Majles representatives who were actually elected through corruption and rigging). However, since a short time ago there was only one well for the men and women to send their messages for Imam, of course after paying the all-important "entrance fee".

But recently the demagogues have separated the line of men and women and now there are two separate wells (channels of communications) with the Hidden Imam in Jamkaran. Every day, a large number of people travel to Jamkaran (a few are true believers but most of them are crooks that want to show off their faith, and there is a third group of the Islamic tourists that go there to kill time).

The income derived from the Hidden Imam's "post office box" is so huge that it covers some of the expenses for the "shadow governments" in Iran. Recently, services of the Jamkaran complex are provided through internet and by e-mail and applicants fill out a form and give their credit card number for a letter to be dropped in the well on their behalf.

LEGACY OF KHOMEINI FOR IRAN: CRUCIFIXION OF IRAN

The current president of Iran has repeatedly said that his policy is going back to the time of Khomeini. He is not alone in feeling nostalgic about going back to the time of Khomeini. Many of the statesmen and Mullahs of the Islamic regime of Iran believe that the words or acts of Khomeini are standards for everything.

These days the mass media of the Iranian Islamic regime is full of materials written by various groups that claim they have understood the messages of Khomeini better than the others. Also you see that many of the same sources in the media criticize each other for failing to observe the sayings of Khomeini. Therefore, it is important and interesting to see what Khomeini was saying and doing when he was alive and ruling Iran.

He came to Iran by lying about his principles, beliefs, and policies. His speeches out of Iran (especially in France) were full of intentionally ambiguous words. His translators added to the confusion by using western style words instead of Khomeini's own words. He was well aware of this fact and never acted to make clarifications. He did not bother to tell the Iranians that he had his own jargon for every aspect of the political affairs.

He was speaking about democracy, national interests, the rights of men and women to live free, economic equality, respect for minorities, and many other issues, but he did not mean what the addressees were thinking. When he was flying to Iran, a journalist asked him: "what is your feeling now that you are going back to Iran". For one minute he was himself. He said: "nothing". He did not really care about Iran; what he had in his mind was serving the ideologies of the Arab nomads of 1400 years ago.

He started deceiving the people right from the start when he set foot in Iran upon his return. He appointed a prime minister and did not grant him any powers. He in fact showed his followers what the meaning of the Islamic-democracy was: to have sham institutions like the Majles, the office of prime minister, ministries and not to give them any power in fact. He invented the ideology of Velayte Faghih to monopolize the power for the Mullahs (even though Beda'at meaning inventing new ideologies is a major sin in Islam) and the concept of Velayate Faghih had no root in any Islamic texts, including Koran.

Economy, under Khomeini, was a mixture of the planned economy of the socialist countries with granting certain Mullahs the freedom to plunder the country. In fact, the economy under Khomeini had all of the negative points of both socialism and market economy, and did not have their positive points. There was no private sector. There was only a Mullah sector in the public and private domain. The prime minister and later the president and government organizations were show figures. They had no real power and they repeated what Khomeini said only using different words. They did not dare to say or act otherwise.

The "culture" at the time of Khomeini was a miserable word. What Khomeini and his associates understood from culture was forcing the people to perform Islamic-Arabic rituals. Although they failed to completely transform Iranians into what they wanted, nevertheless Iranians have suffered and continue to suffer from the ideas of the great demagogue. The regime headed by Khomeini, ordered that art be at the service of the Islamic ideology. They changed the name of the Ministry of Culture to the Ministry of Islamic Guidance. The duty of the ministry was to suppress the freedoms of speech, expression and religion.

Khomeini's policy about the hostage taking issue in the occupied American Embassy in Tehran was interesting. He did not know anything about the issue and he decided to reject it. However, when the so-called students that had occupied the American Embassy told him that they could pretend to have found many things against his enemies, he started to support them. His policy ended up costing Iran dearly for many aspects.

Khomeini's policy during the Iran-Iraq war was horrible. He acted as a bloodthirsty mad dog. While the people of Iran were being killed by the thousands due to the policy of human waves, he insisted on the point that Saddam should be eliminated. Ironically, Khomeini who kept saying Saddam won't last died before Saddam.

Khomeini kept contradicting himself during different speeches in a day or even in the same sermon and never acknowledged or tried to rectify these mistakes. In one breath he was telling the people that "America can't do a damn thing." and at the same time he claimed that every problem that was happening in Iran was due to American policies. Saddam was attacking Iranian cities with Russian aircrafts and rockets but Khomeini was busy shouting slogans against the USA (interestingly, the bulk of weapons in Saddam's army was Russian, unlike the Iranian army's weapons which was almost completely American).

Khomeini's legacy in the prisons of Iran was also terrible. He said "the prisons must turn into universities". In fact, the prisons, headed by persons like Assadollah Lajevardi, the Butcher of Evin, turned into killing fields. Thousands of Iranians were tortured and killed in prisons for trying to have political freedom or express their views. At the end of Iran-Iraq war, according to his direct instructions, more than 8 thousand prisoners were killed in a couple of days in the so-called "universities of Khomeini".

He said that the income from oil would be distributed equally. What he did in action was permitting the Mullahs to spend the oil income in whatever way they wanted. In a couple of years, the Mullahs who used to live mostly like the lowest classes of the people turned into wealthy people. Some of the Mullahs became billionaires. Some of the Mullahs and their apprentices who used to go to people's houses and give useless lectures (usually in the funerals) turned into ideologues, members of Majles, ambassadors and so on.

The religious students in the theological centers which were the centers of poverty, corruption, and "backwardness", turned into "Ulama" or the "scholars". Khomeini thought these "students" will be physicians, engineers, and so on overnight but in fact they just remained religious students. These students ruined the sciences and everything connected to them. The number of the religious students increased in a massive way due to all kinds of advantages and concessions they received from the government.

The ordinary schools were turned into centers for brainwashing. The history books were contaminated and distorted. The students were given more credits according to their progress in learning the religious oriented books and attention to the sciences was reduced to zero. The Universities were closed for several years under the pretext of the Cultural Revolution and when they reopened all of the professors were thrown out.

An institution called "Tarbiyate Moddarress" was established to mass-produce "professors" for the Iranian universities. The new "professors" were chosen from the lowest level of the university graduates (usually in the BA and BS level). This new breed of the so-called "professors" brought down the level of higher education in Iran. On every occasion when the government makes a policy or says something according to the interpretations of the Islamic regime, these "professors" and "scientists" try to justify the government's position by stating that they are right.

The policy of Khomeini in the Persian Gulf was turning the Persian Gulf into the Islamic Gulf. In the Caspian Sea, they chose to keep quiet about whatever the Russians said. In the Chechen, they acted as if the Muslims of the former USSR and present Russian Federation did not exit.

At the same time, Khomeini announced a day for commemoration of the Palestinians, gave them money, and invited Arafat to Tehran and kissed him many times. Khomeini tried to turn the issue of Palestine into an important issue for the life of Iranians, while most of Iranians did not care to know where Palestine was.

Khomeini confiscated the companies and production facilities and service units all over Iran. He gave those companies and factories which made a profit to the Mullahs and the rest were gathered in an organization called "the National Industries of Iran." Gradually, many of the profitable companies became bankrupt due to the plundering of Mullahs, mismanagement and corruption and they joined the "National Industries of Iran".

They established revolutionary courts on the basis of the rules of the Arab nomads of 1400 years ago and appointed some of the most cruel and criminal Mullahs as judges. The Mullahs who did not know anything about the rights of the people became the judges. They used Khomeini's books (usually written in Arabic and some were translated into Farsi) as the sources of law.

The women were covered, ousted from many posts, persuaded to stay home and give birth to as many children as they could. Family planning collapsed in Iran and rapid growth of population damaged the country.

Khomeini did not speak Farsi well; for example, he put the subject and verb in the wrong places and used indicative pronouns (like this and that) in a way that was confusing and showed his lack of skill in the Persian language. He used some Arabic words in his Farsi speeches that were outdated even for the Arabs. He sounded in some cases like Yoda in Star Wars. Those who have collected his words in several books most of which is meaningless have corrected some of the sentences. In recent years, some of speeches of Khomeini, especially his famous sermon upon entry to Iran, which he delivered it in Beheshet Zahra Cemetery, are materials that is no longer distributed or published because they clearly demonstrate the depth of deception and treachery in his words. Some of the collections of his speeches are not available easily because they contain so many contradictory ideas and those speeches are even opposed by the people in power.

It is interesting that some Iranian ghost writers and poets have attributed poems, in the style of Hafez, to Khomeini. Of course, no other explanation would make sense because it would be a miracle for a person who did not know basic Farsi grammar to produce such elaborate poems.

The collection of the words of Khomeini, published in hundreds of volumes, show how shallow his understanding was of the political and international situations. He has given wrong directions and taken things out of context.

He has given wrong statistics, made serious mistakes in judgment about important and unimportant issues and suppressed the national feeling of Iranians, and tried to prove his obedience to the nomadic Arabs of 1400 years ago. Yet some of the Iranian Islamic zealots think that his words are more important than Koran. As it was mentioned, the judges in the Islamic Revolutionary Courts of Iran deliver rulings on the basis of those words and refer to the collection of Khomeini's words as the source of law.

The shameful era of Khomeini is over and yet some idiots like the president of Iran wish to go back to those days. The current president, like many others, will understand soon that he is wrong, but unfortunately the people of Iran have to pay the price for him to learn his lesson on the job.

Differences between the Government and the People of Iran

The governments of the countries in the present world represent their people to varying degrees. The dictatorial systems are the least transparent regimes and you never know what percentage of the people really support the government. However, in one dictatorial regime, which is in power in Iran, the distinction between the regime and the people is very clear.

This distinction is important for many purposes:

1- The people of Iran are not responsible for the policies of the regime (such as wiping out Israel, sending money and weapons for Palestinians, opposing all Western notions, supporting the nomadic Arab laws and so on). The people of the other countries must take notice of this distinction and not treat Iranians as people who support the policies of the regime.

2- The other governments must note that the Iranian government does not represent the people of Iran and they should treat the regime as an institution opposing the people

3- The people of Iran, unlike the regime that rules the country through the Mafia of Velayate-Faghigh (government of Mullahs), do not like to live and act like the ancient nomadic Arabs and there is no wish among the people to revive the laws of the nomadic Arabs of 1400 years ago.

4- The people of Iran, unlike the Islamic regime of Iran, do not like to look like terrorists, support or glorify the acts of terrorism at any level. It is wrong to treat the Iranian people as the nation of terrorists. It is ridiculous that the agents of the Islamic regime of Iran, including the Mullahs and their lackeys travel with diplomatic immunity and diplomatic passport everywhere including the USA (The top criminal Mullahs of Iran, like Messabah Yazdi, the ideologue of violence and the spiritual father of the president of Iran, is a frequent visitor to the USA. His son has recently immigrated to Canada), and the ordinary people of Iran who have nothing to do with the policies of the regime are subjected to many difficulties.

It is time that the officials of all countries, including officials at places like the airports and such draw a clear distinction between the people of Iran and the regime of Iran. In the case of the Islamic Republic of Iran, there are so many differences between the regime governing the country and the people of Iran that you can easily make the distinction. The government of the Islamic regime of Iran represents less than 10 percent of the people. Even this ten percent do not really support the regime. It is just in their interest to pretend to do so for the time being. The people who have been given housing by being placed in the houses illegally confiscated by the so-called Islamic courts, are very well aware that if they miss one pro-government demonstration ordered by the Supreme Leader, they are going to end up in the street the next day. The Basijis (these are street thugs that act as the religious vigilantes who were used in the wartime as "disposable" items. Sometimes they were sent along with domestic animals over the mine fields before the Revolutionary Guards staged their attack) who have entered the university without going through the difficult university entrance examinations (the test called Kounkor, like conquer), know that if they do not take part in attacking the other students in the universities or if they fail to threaten the academicians to stay in the governmental lines, they are going to return to the previous status: working as simple construction worker.

5. The people of Iran and the present government differ in one significant way. The People of Iran are not seriously religious, they do not like the expansion of Islam in Iran, they are in love with progress, they love the USA, and many Iranians inside Iran when they talk about going to a foreign country they mean the USA. The Iranians in other places are only on their way to the USA or something similar. USA is the final destination of many Iranians. The people of Iran do not care about the Muslims in other countries, especially Palestine, Chechen, Saudi Arabia and so on. The people of Iran wish to live in peace with all other nations and try to get to the highest scientific level which is clearly reflected by the extremely high number of the Iranians in the academic and scientific positions in the most advanced countries of the world.

On the other side, the regime of the Islamic Republic of Iran is dreaming about the expansion of Islam (as the limited ideology of Shiites), expanding Arabic words, including the Arab nomads' law in the Iranian laws, especially when it comes to criminal law and women's rights. For example, in the Islamic criminal codes murder is considered as a personal thing. If the next of kin forgives the murderer, he or she is free to go. If a father kills his son, there are no murder charges. It is a source of embarrassment for the society of Iran, which is more advanced than many other third world countries, that its judicial system is based on the laws of 1400 years ago of the nomad Arabs. The people of Iran certainly do not like this and the government that imposes such laws on the people of Iran is very far from representing them.

The government and the people of Iran differ in the fields of politics, economy, foreign relations, nuclear energy, terrorism, and so on. The Iranian people have a long history and are proud of that. The government of Iran acts as if Iran was born after the invasion of the Arabs against Iran. The Iranian people are proud that they have had literary figures like Saadi, Hafez , Ferdowsi and Forooghe Faraokhzad in the past, and the Iranian regime acts as if they do not exist when these figures speak about love, sex and humanity.

The Iranian people are respectful of the Universal Declaration of Human Rights (and the International Conventions on the Civil, Political, Economic and Social Rights), and the government of Iran is trying to replace them with what it calls Islamic human rights which a collection of outdated rules of the nomadic Arabs of 1400 years ago. The people of Iran do not consider women as the property of men, and government of Iran, which is not ready to accept women as human beings (and for the same reason refrains from adhering to the United Nations Convention on Elimination of All kinds of Discriminations Against Women), considers women as inferior persons and something like slaves.

The people of Iran are happy to celebrate their historical occasions such as Nowruz, Sizdahbedar, Charshanbesoori, Sadeh, Mehreghan and others, but the government of Iran undermines those celebrations by not allowing them under the guise of keeping order.

The people of Iran, unlike the government of Iran, do not care really when a couple of ancient Arab tribesmen killed each other to get political power under the name of Islam 1400 years ago. The heroes of the Iranian people are Rostam and Jamshid, Feraydoun, Bahman, Gordafarid, Tahmineh and so on and the government of Iran is after several Arab figures that Iranians do not know almost anything about.

The people of Iran, unlike the government are not afraid of men and women shaking hands and men looking at women who are not wearing Islamic head scarf. The people of Iran see nothing wrong with men and women gathering in parties, reciting poems, dancing, and mingling, but the government of Iran thinks this is criminal act. The people of Iran think that they should be able to have a couple of beers and live decently, but the government of Iran thinks this is criminal behavior that calls for lashing.

The people of Iran oppose the occupation of the American Embassy in Tehran and look forward to the day the American Embassy is re-opened in Iran, but the government of Iran celebrates the date of occupation and has appointed the criminals who did this act as Iranian ambassadors in the foreign countries.

The Iranian people, unlike the regime, do not consider the 12th of February (22nd of Bahman) as the day of Revolution; the people think of this date as the day that the Mullahs deceived the Iranian people. This is the National Deception Date and it will remain as an embarrassing point in Iran's history, comparable to the date that Rostame Faraokhzad, the commander of the Iranian forces, lost the war to a group of nomadic Arabs that were determined to get their hands on the wealth and civilization of Iran. Unfortunately these Arabs succeeded to capture and redistribute Iranian culture and civilization as their own. However they never succeeded to eradicate the identity of Iranians (as they did in places like Egypt). The people of Iran dream of a world in peace and progress, but the regime of Iran dreams of domination of its retarded ideology over the world. The people of Iran have the greatest level of tolerance towards all other religious minorities and racial groups, but the narrow-minded regime of Iran is not able to tolerate even the offspring of its own ideology. The people of Iran, unlike the government of Mullahs, have no problem with women taking part in all fields of sports and watch sporting events as they like. The people of Iran, unlike the regime of Mullahs, do not agree with the hallucinations of Ahmadinejad, who is imposed on the people of Iran as the president through sham elections and the Mafia of the ruling Mullahs.

The people of Iran, unlike the regime of the Islamic Republic of Iran, do not agree with the activities of the revolutionary and paramilitary forces of Iran that act like an Army of Occupation in Iran. The people of Iran, unlike the government, are proud that in Iran's history there were women who reached the level of the Head of the State, long before many other nations and at a time when the ancient nomadic Arabs buried their new-born girls alive (the Prophet of the ancient Arabs asked them to stop this practice. This is mentioned as a glory point for the human rights in the history of Islam.)

Those who do not differentiate between the people of Iran and the Islamic regime of Iran (whether they be politicians, journalists, or ordinary people) run the risk of reaching contradictory and unreasonable results and analyses about the situation of Iran.

CHARACTERISTICS OF THE ALTERNATIVE TO THE ISLAMIC REGIME OF IRAN THE EXPERIENCE OF ISLAMIC

The Islamic revolution in Iran proved once again that mixture of politics and Islam in a world that is divided into nation-states and the governments designed to follow the national interests does not work. For a long time in Iran (hundreds of years), religious people had claimed that all problems in society came from non-observance of Islamic rules and if religious Islamic leaders become political masters in society, everything would be in order and justice would prevail all over the state. More than two decades of Islamic government in Iran has shown clearly that the idea is not working.

There is no doubt that the people of Iran are less religious and more under-developed now, compared to thirty years ago. The Iranian experience had a great deal of impact on many Muslim countries. The tide of Islamic revolutions in all these countries has died. The Islamic revolution should have happened in countries like Egypt and Algeria much sooner than Iran because their people were more prone to accepting Islamic tenets. Now, the experience of the Iranian revolution has discouraged them from moving in the same line. At the moment, no great Islamic revolution is in the making.

On the other hand, many people in all Islamic societies are trying to separate religion from politics. What is happening in Iran at the present juncture is a clear struggle by the people of Iran to separate religion from politics. There is no other way. Anyone, including all Muslims and any government, especially the U.S. which wish a better life for the people of Islamic countries and similar states, and also seek international peace and development should help the cause of separating religion from politics. At the same time, one of the most important points that have helped the present regime of Iran, with all its incompetence and unskillful management, to remain in power is the discussion about the alternative. As soon as the discussion begins about the shortages and problems of the present regime, the question comes to mind as to what is the alternative to the present regime of Iran? Who are the forces that are or claim to be the opposition? Which of them is proper for popular support? I do not have a clear response to that question. But here are the characteristics of the future government of Iran. The future regime of Iran (whatever it is called) must have the following characteristics:

(1) Secularism. This means that the people are sick and tired of religious extremism. Religion is a personal thing and it should not be run by the government. Imposing ideas is against the freedom of expression and a violation of the people's basic rights. Religion should be separated from the state. A special organization should be established to look for and discard religious notions that find their way into state affairs.

(2) The revival of the Iranian identity- the present religious government of Iran has been trying to disconnect Iranians from their glorious past. Although Iranians have received Islam through Arabs, this is not something the Iranians appreciate or welcome. Many Iranians still feel the humiliation of an imposed religion. Some Iranians believe that Islam was planted by the Iranians in the Arabia, which was part of the lands ruled by Sasanid and other Iranian dynasties. Also a number of Iranians believe that what we hear about great Islamic civilization is in fact the Iranian rich heritage captured and redistributed by Arabs who lived in nomadic tribes of Arabia at the advent of Islam. Contrary to

what may Westerners think, Iran is not an Arab country and it is not a deeply Islamic country. The people of Iran are not serious Muslims and they do not intend to be so. Unfortunately, the present Government of Iran that does not represent the people of Iran has taken positions that are against the Iranian ideas and interests.

(3) Respecting human rights as mentioned in the Universal Declaration of Human Rights. The new government of Iran should observe the Universal Declaration of Human rights and should respect the obligations accepted by the state of Iran regarding the United Nations Covenant on the Civil and Political Rights and also the UN Covenant on the Economic Rights.

(4) Equality of women in all aspects with men as a principle. Islamic rules, as interpreted by many Islamic experts are against the equality of men and women. There are many points that differ in Islam and the UN Convention on Eradication of All Forms of Discrimination against Women. It goes without saying that women as equals have all of the rights that men enjoy. The nomadic norms of the ancient Arabs cannot be the basis of law in a modern nation-state. The Islamic rules about women should be discarded totally as they are against the human rights and human dignity.

(5) The government must be elected. The people of Iran like almost all peoples in the world are seeking a democracy for their country. They have been struggling for this purpose during the last hundred years. Iranian people reached the conclusion of the need for democracy far earlier than many other nations. Unfortunately, the efforts of Iranian people for getting to democracy have been undermined by various internal and external elements. The 1979 Revolution in Iran was one of the latest efforts of this nation to get democracy but again it has been deviated by a minority of religiously narrow-minded persons.

(6) Changing the Iranian calendar to an Iranian form. It is meaningless for Iranians to choose something in the Arab history as the basis of Iranian history. The Iranians had a great civilization before the developments in the Arab regions and something like

the date of the first universal declaration of human rights issued by Cyrus the Great must be the basis for the Iranian calendar. This is a necessary goal for the new regime.

(7) Free economy based on the market and governmental supervision. Centralized economy is a bad idea. Iran has suffered a lot due to the economic policies of the religious zealots who have tried to impose the Marxist economy under Islamic disguise. The new regime of Iran must stay away from centralized economy.

(8) No interest in the issues of Arabs and the Palestine. Iranians do not care what the issue of Palestine is. The Arabs for their part have had many negative approaches toward Iran. Apart from the fact that the Arabs called the Iranian Muslims Ajam (aliens) or Majous (Zoroastrians), the Arabs held Iranians responsible for the biggest division in Islam. Sometimes Iranians are called Rafezi (meaning those who are far from the religion of Islam or they have left the religion). Even today, some groups, like the followers of various factions in Iraq constantly call the Shiites of Iran as Rafezi. In fact Arabs also do not want interference of Iran in their affairs like the case of Palestine.

(9) Good relations with the West especially the USA. Iran and the USA have many common interests. Iran can get its proper position in the region and the world through cooperation with the USA. Just imagine what will happen in the case of Iranian rights in the Caspian Sea and the Persian Gulf if the USA is on the Iranian side.

(10) National reconciliation. Many of the people who work with the present regime of Iran are forced to do so for survival. The new regime or the alternative to the Islamic regime must have enough capacity for a national reconciliation in order to avoid bloodshed and use all forces for the development of the country. Also, a merit system must be established. The Islamic Republic of Iran has introduced the system of blind obedience and has imposed it in all levels. Illiteracy and ignorance are top qualities for the managers of the Islamic government in Iran. This must give way to a merit system.

BAD MANAGEMENT IN IRAN

The Iranian regime suffers from a weakness called: "Bazari management" (Modiryat-e Hojreie). This is due to the nature of many managers who have the same background, such as:

1. Poor education. The managers of the Islamic Republic of Iran, even those who claim o have advanced degrees suffer from poor education. These managers, in the process of their studies, have concentrated more on the issues like activities in the ideological gatherings which are unrelated to their studies as compared to academic activities. These managers, whether inside or outside of the country, have studied and worked in an isolated manner so you will see that the managers (like the current Iranian Minister of Foreign Affairs, Motaki) who have supposedly studied many years abroad and in the English-speaking communities can hardly speak a word of English. They have no understanding of the culture of societies in which they have lived. Due to a large Iranian community living out of Iran, many of the Islamic managers spend all of their time during their study period abroad among the friends and families with similar convictions. Bazari Iranians love to send their children out of the country for education (especially when they fail in the entrance examinations of the Iranian universities)

and at the same time, they do everything possible to stop their children from learning the language and culture of the host countries. Therefore, failure to understand others be it in or out of the country is a common weakness among the Islamic managers.

2. Religious conviction. The Iranian mangers of the Islamic regime have an Islamic conviction that relies on God for the outcome of the actions. They try to act as they think the Islamic religion wants them to act and they do not care what happens next. They think that God has the ultimate responsibility and this is why they never doubt their ability to run any establishment in any capacity until of course they are kicked out of power. Khomeini once asked the Islamic regime's managers to resign if they believed they were not suited for the job, but no one resigned. Not even the street sweeper resigned.

3. Bazari roots. Bazar, or the small and big trading centers in Iran, has always been the greatest supporter of the Islamic revolution in Iran. The Bazaris played a great role in paying the expenses of the Mullahs for coming into power in Iran (they paid for Khomeini's charter flight from France to Iran). They have always been paying a special tax called the "share of Imam" to the religious leaders but they have always evaded paying legitimate taxes to the government authorities. The Islamic regime uses a large number of the Bazaris and their off springs in management of the country. The special characteristics of Bazari businessmen are quite evident in the decision-making and management skills of these persons. The Bazari mentality is dominant in all organizations of the Islamic regime.

4. Shortsightedness is a weakness from which the Islamic managers of the Iranian regime suffer. They survive day by day. They do not any skills for long-term planning because they do not see that far into the future and they do not think strategically. They live for today and at most, for tomorrow.

5. Ignoring the interests of the others is a big problem for the Bazari management. They think only about their own interests and they believe if they are in the position of power or wealth, God has given it to them based on some divine calculations and by the same token if others are disadvantaged, they must be suffering based on a divine plan.

6. Black market skills are a result of the Bazari type of life. Bazaris have always had a two-sided life in Iran: over the table and under the table. The black market in the Iranian Bazar is always bigger than and more lucrative than the official market. Sometimes the official market is only a showcase. For example, you see a small shop in Bazar that apparently sells scarves, but actually the shop is engaged in money laundering, foreign exchange and gold coins. There are thousands of similar businesses in Bazar. The mangers coming from Bazar do not consider corruption, nepotism, double standards, under the carpet dealings as negative and routinely utilize the same in their management.

7. Changing their minds as quickly as it suits their purpose is a characteristic of the Bazari managers. They change their views as often as needed and they do not care about the consequences. They have the large army of Mullahs to play the role of the spin-doctors for them. For example, you place a Bazari manager in charge of building a dam but he is for some reason unable to deliver on the promise, so he quickly comes up with reasons why it was not a good idea to begin with while the real reason for failure of the project may in fact be a direct result of poor management.

8. Treating employees as apprentices or even slaves is a deep-rooted Bazari tradition. The Bazari managers do not consider the people who work under them worthy of serious consultation or management participation. The employees are apprentices under the training of the

Islamic manager and they remain as such until the manager decides otherwise. The Bazari manager believes he is entitled to throw an employee out of the organization for even the smallest infraction and feels no responsibility for the impact on the employee's life.

9. The Islamic managers of the regime feel that they are the top thinkers and they are highly intelligent or born to be leaders. This arrogance is evident in all of their moves. They always appear to be very calm and they even smile when they are talking about important issues. This condescending smile is intended to give the impression that they know many things that are over the audience's head, but the reality is that they are hiding behind a wall of ignorance and arrogance.

10. The Bazari's view of women is always very close to the Islamic rules. Sometimes you feel that the Islamic rules are written for Bazaris only (after all, the prophet of Islam was also a Bazari meaning a merchant). The Bazaris' view of women's right and their level of respect for women do not allow them to consider women as suitable for important positions out of the house.

THE ROLE OF HIDDEN IMAM IN THE HISTORY AND THE POLITICS OF THE ISLAMIC REPUBLIC OF IRAN

The notion of the Hidden Imam (Islamic Messiah) has a central role in the Islamic Shiite thoughts. There are countless references to the Hidden Imam in the Shiite books. However, following the victory of the so-called Islamic Revolution in Iran (or as some people say: the hijacking of the Iranian revolution by the Mullahs), in 1979, the references to the Hidden Imam has gained new importance.

The main reason for this is that the power and wealth of an important oil-exporting contrary, with a tyrannical regime that does not care about the wishes of its people has been directed in support of the old religious notions. This does not mean that everybody in Iran or the Shiite world agrees on the role and modus operandi of the Hidden Imam. In fact, Khomeini, the so-called founder of the Islamic Revolution in Iran stopped the activities of one of the most important groups that claimed to be the strict follower of the Hidden Imam. This group was called Hojjatieh.

Since the election of Mahmud Ahmadinejad as the president of Iran through rigged elections, the notion of the Hidden Imam has gained new weight. Many of the actions of the present government of Iran seem to have originated from the same notion.

For example the first letter of Ahmadinejad to President Bush was not based on political considerations (it was written at the worst possible time given the existing political atmosphere), and it did not mean to change anything about the most important current issue of Iran (the nuclear case of Iran and the sanctions through the United Nations Security Council).

The president of Iran thinks that he has a divine duty from the Hidden Imam to take certain measures and the letter to President Bush was supposed to be one of these measures. Anybody inside and outside of Iran trying to explain the letter from a political and international aspect is on the wrong track and will come to the wrong conclusion.

Sayyed Vahid Karimi, who is introduced as strategic issues researcher in Iran, has said: "we have a duty to guide this ignorant superpower [the USA]." (1) He has recommended that such letters should be sent to the leaders of the important states in the world, including the UK. It is therefore important to know in more details on what is the notion of the Hidden Imam and its role in the present government of Iran.

Who is the Hidden Imam? According to Richard Hines (2): "The core of the Shi'ite religious world view is the Hidden Imam, Muhammad al-Mahdi, "The Guided One." While the stories of the first eleven Imams are historical in nature, the history of the twelfth Imam is mystical and miraculous. Born in 868 AD / 255 AH, Abu'l-Kasim Muhammad (which is the name of the Prophet himself), and when Hasan al-Askari, the Eleventh Imam, died in 874 AD / 260 AH, the seven year old boy declared himself to be the Twelfth Imam and went into hiding. The Shi'ites believed that he hid himself in a cave below a mosque in Samarra; this cave is blocked by a gate which the Shi'ites call Bab-al Ghayba, or the "Gate of Occultation." This is one of the most sacred sites in Shi'a Islam, and the faithful gather here to pray for the return of the Twelfth Imam. The central Shi'a doctrines revolving around the Hidden Imam are the doctrines of Occultation (Ghayba) and Return (Raj'a) .

The Doctrine of Occultation is simply the belief that God hid Muhammad al-Mahdi away from the eyes of men in order to preserve his life. God has miraculously kept him alive since the day he was hidden in 874 AD / 260 AH; eventually God will reveal al-Mahdi to the world and he will return to guide humanity.

The Occultation has two distinct stages, the Lesser Occultation and the Greater Occultation. In the Lesser Occultation, the Hidden Imam continued to communicate with humanity through representatives. Since the Imam was the spiritual guide or light to the rest of humanity, the Lesser Occultation only removed the Imam's body from the world, not his spiritual guidance. However, under the threat of orthodox Muslims, the Hidden Imam entered the period of Greater Occultation, which is still continuing.

In the Greater Occultation, the Imam is still the spiritual guide and light of the world with one exception: there is no longer any direct communication between humanity and the Imam...."

Names and Characteristics of the Hidden Imam According to the Encyclopedia of the Orient (3): "Muhammad al Mahdi (the guided) is the 12th and last Imam of the Twelver Shi'i, and is also known as Muhammad al Muntazar (the awaited). Very little can be said of him with any certainty. In fact, the non-Twelver might very well question whether there was an historical person associated with the name. Jafar, the brother of the Eleventh Imam denied the existence of any child and claimed the Imamate for himself. In fact, accounts of public appearances by Muhammad al Mahdi often involve his mysterious arrival at key moments to challenge his uncle's claims.

In brief, the Twelver Shi'i believe that he was born to a Byzantine slave named Narjis Khatun, and that his birth was kept quiet by his father, the Eleventh Imam, Hassan al Askari, because of the intense persecution of the Shi'is at that time. Hidden since birth, he reappeared at age of 6 to assert his claim to the Imamate, only to then disappear down a well to avoid the sad fate of his father and grandfather.

For the next seventy years he maintained contact with his followers through a succession of four assistants, each known as

Bab (Gate), Uthman al Amir; his son Abu Jafar Muhammad ibn Uthman; Abu'l Qasim Husayn ibn Ruh an Nawbakhti; and Abu'l Husayn Ali ibn Muhammad as-Samarri. The period when he used the 4 Babs as his form of contacting the Shi'is is known as the Lesser Occultation. On his deathbed in 941 CE, the fourth Bab, as-Samarri produced a letter from the Imam stating that there should be no successor to as-Samarri and that from that time forward the Mahdi would not be seen until he reappeared as champion of the faithful in the events leading to the Judgment Day.

Therefore, after 941 CE there has been no earthly expression of the Imamate. This period is known as the Greater Occultation. However, it is still possible to seek the Twelfth Imam's advice or intercession by writing him a letter and leaving it at one of the Shi'i shrines... There is much that is miraculous associated with al Mahdi. The various traditions are rich in stories and are often contradictory.

Tales range from speaking from the womb, growing at so aston-ishing a rate that he was full grown by age 6, being raised by birds and with the ability to appear and disappear at will. While there was much controversy over the succession of the 12th Imam, as the Lesser Occultation proceeded, dissent gradually dimin-ished. This can be attributed in part to the active support of the Caliphate for the institution of the Bab. Several opponents of the doctrine of the Occultation were executed and others were persecuted in various ways.

Another factor explaining the acceptance of the Lesser Occulta-tion, and by extension the Greater Occultation, was that due to the house arrest of the 10th and 11th Imams. Hence, most Shi'is were already accustomed to the idea of their Imam being hid-den from their view. In the time of the 10th and 11th Imams, a network of wikala (agents) had developed to act as intermediar-ies between the Imam and his followers, handling money and carrying messages back and forth. In fact, Uthman al Amri, the first Bab of the 12th Imam had held the same position as head of the wikala under the 11th Imam. Therefore, for most Shi'i, there was not a significant change in their relation to their Imam after the death of the Eleventh Imam. Some titles of the 12th Imam include: Sahib az Zaman (Master of the Age), Sahib al Amr (Master of Command), al Qa'im (the one to arise), Baqiyyat Allah (remnant of Allah) and Imam al Muntazar (the awaited Imam)."

Signs of Hidden Imam's Appearance

Gregoire de Kalbermatten (4) has mentioned the signs of the appearance of Mahdi: "The universal precursory Sign of the return of the Mahdi, "He who Guides," consists of the general invasion of the earth by Evil and the victory of the forces of Evil over those of Good. Without such a manifestation, the entirety of humanity would be engulfed by darkness.... The Sign consists of the following traits: the people will neglect prayer, squander the divinity which is conferred on them, legalize untruths, practice usury, accept bribes, construct huge edifices, sell religion to win this lower world, employ idiots, consult with women, break family ties, obey passion and consider insignificant the letting of blood. Magnanimity will be considered as weakness and injustice as glory, princesses will be debauched and ministers will be oppressors, intellectuals will be traitors and the reader of the Koran vicious. False witness will be brought openly and immorality proclaimed in loud voices.

A word of promise will be slander, sin and exaggeration. "The sacred Books will be ornate, the mosques disguised, the minarets extended. Criminals will be praised, the lines of combat narrowed, hearts in disaccord and pacts broken. Women, greedy for the riches of this lower world, will involve themselves in the business of their husbands; the vicious voices of the man will be loud and will be listened to. The most ignoble of the people will become leaders, the debauched will be believed for fear of the Evil they will cause, the liar will be considered as truthful and the traitor as trustworthy... They will resort to singers and musical instruments ... and women will horse ride, they will resemble men and the men will resemble women. The people will prefer the activities of this lower-world to those of the Higher-World and will cover with lambskin the hearts of wolves."

Dajjal or the Islamic anti-Christ

Dajjal is an important notion, which is related to the concept of the Hidden Imam. On the basis of the Shiit teachings, Dajjal will appear right before the Hidden Imam and he will try to deceive people by pretending to be the Hidden Imam. He is later killed by "Jesus Christ" who will return to earth and pave the way for the Hidden Imam. Christ will fight along with the Hidden Imam for a while, and during this time all Christians become Muslims and later he leaves the scene completely for the Hidden Imam.

Mohammed Ali Ibn Zubair Ali (5) describes Dajjal or the Islamic Anti-Christ as: "...He will emerge between Shaam [Syria] and Iraq, and his emergence will become known when he is in Isfahaan [central Iran] at a place called Yahudea [the Jews Place]. The Yahudis (Jews) of Isfahaan will be his main followers. Apart from having mainly Yahudi followers, he will have a great number of women followers as well... There will be a thick fingernail-like object in his left eye. The letters "Kaa" "Faa" "Raa" will appear on his forehead and will be deciphered by all Mu'mineen whether or not they are literate.

He will have a wheatish complexion. He will travel at great speed and his means of conveyance will be a gigantic mule. It is said that he will play beautiful music which will attract the music lovers. Dajjal will lay claim to prophethood. He will then lay claim to Divinity. He will perform unusual feats. He will travel the entire world...The hidden treasures will spill forth at his command. He will stay on this Earth for a period of forty days; the length of the first day will be one year, the second day will be equal to one month, the third day will be equal to a week and the remaining days will be normal..."

Mosque in Jamkaran of Iran

In the Persian Journal I wrote (6): Jamkaran is a village near Qom in the South of Tehran. It is the home for a lucrative business of corresponding with the Imam e Zaman or the Hidden Imam or the Islamic Messiah. According to the Islamic-Shiite stories, Imam e Zaman will appear and enforce justice all over the world.

The Shiites have been waiting for his appearance in the last 14 centuries. Again according to the Islamic-Shiite stories, anyone who wants to send a letter to the Imam e Zaman can write it and throw it in any flowing underground current or well.

Also, Jackson Diehl, reporting from Qom in Iran says (7): " in a dusty village outside this Shiite holy city, a once-humble yellow-brick mosque is undergoing a furious expansion.... the expansion is driven by an apocalyptic vision: that Shiite Islam's long-hidden 12th Imam, or Madhi, will soon emerge - possibly at the Mosque of Jamkaran- to inaugurate the end of the world. The man who provided $20 million to prepare the shrine for that moment, the Iranian President Mahmud Ahmadinejad, has reportedly told his cabinet that he expects the Mahdi to arrive within the next two years..."

Hojjatieh and the Hidden Imam

In an article regarding the "Hojjatieh Group", the newspaper published by the exiled former president of Iran, Abulhasan Bani Sadr (8) has mentioned: "during the elections for the Seventh Majles, the Hojjatieh elements played an important role and they sent their agents inside the Majles under the disguise of "fundamentalism".

Also, Meshkini (the former Friday Prayer leader of Qom), claimed that the Hidden Imam had endorsed the list of the Majles deputies for the Seventh Majles. Later, during the presidential elections, Mesbah Yazdi, claimed that someone in Ahwaz had seen the Hidden Imam in his dreams who had prayed for success of "Ahmadinejad" [the current president of Iran] in the elections. This opened the hands of the Hojjatieh mules in the Islamic Revolutionary Guards and other organizations for propaganda in favor of Ahmadinejad and rigging the elections in his support.

At the moment, Ahmadinejad and his ministers claim that they get instructions from the Hidden Imam directly...in the first session of the Council of the Ministers, Ahmadinejad and his ministers signed a treaty with the Hidden Imam and they asked Sadr Harandi, the Minister of Culture, to hand over the treaty to the

Hidden Imam by throwing a copy of the Treaty down the well in Jamkaran. In the second session of the Council of Ministers, Rahmati, the Minister of Roads and Transportation said: "due to the high amount of donations to Jamkaran, we do not need to set aside a governmental budget for construction of the Tehran-Jamkaran railway." Ahmadinejad answered him with anger: "we have not come [to power] for democracy. We are here to prepare the way for the emergence of the Hidden Imam.... " These are some of the convictions of the Mafia that Ahmadinejad represents:

* The Hidden Imam is present in many places

* All preparations must be made for his emergence

* Some of the members of the group have met the prophet and his companions

* When they perform the prayer called "Tavassol" [which calls for the emergence of the hidden Imam], the Imam comes to the session

* They claim to be chosen as the companions of the Hidden Imam and at least some of them are among the 313 special persons or even the 10 prominent persons that will fight along with the Hidden Imam.

* They claim that the Hidden Imam has given presents to some of them

* They claim that they get the solution to the problems from the Hidden Imam

* They believe that the Hidden Imam will appear in the next couple of years...they have established organizations to find the proper persons to fight along the army of the Hidden Imam

* They claim to be protected by the Hidden Imam

* They oppose Bahai Faith and Sunnis

Notes:

(1) http://www.iranpressnews.com/print-me.php dated 10 May 2006.

(2) http://www.wsu.edu/-dee/SHIA/HIDDEM.HTM, dated 6/6/1996)

(3) Muhammad Al Mahdi, Encyclopedia of the Orient, http://I-cias.com/e.o/12thimam.htm.

(4) Gregoire DE Kalbermatten, the Third Advent, King Printing 3003. p.205, (http://www.al-qiyamah.org/hidden_imam_mahdi_(qaf).htm).

(5) "Signs of Qiyamah" by Mohammed Ali Ibn Zubair Ali, http://www.islam.te/prophecies/masdaj.html

(6) Interesting businesses in the Islamic Republic of Iran, Bahman Aghai Diba, the Persian Journal, Nov. 8, 2005

(7) Jackson Diehl Washington Post, May 11, 2006, P.A27, "In Iran, Apocalypse vs. reform"

(8) Enghelab-e Eslami (In Persian), http://news.gooya.com/politics/archives/041779.php dated 4 Jan. 2006

Is Iranian regime ready for the great bargain with the USA?

The Islamic Republic of Iran has been engaged in numerous small and big cases of negotiations during the last quarter of century. Many of these have proceeded in the ordinary pattern of the diplomatic negotiations and they involved ordinary methods of "quid pro quo" (this for that). However, there are several important cases that reveal the way the Iranian regime responds to pressures for compromise in very important issues:

* The American hostages in Iran

* Termination of the Iran-Iraq War

*The proposals of Iran in 2003

* The nuclear case

The American hostages in Iran - in the hostage case, Iran could get many advantages from the Carter Administration before it was forced to release the diplomats and sign the Algiers Declarations. The regime of Iran waited 444 days and eventually under the threats of the new US administration, it accepted the "Declaration of Algiers".

This document is a "treaty" and the title of "Declaration" is only a cover. It is interesting that the Iranian negotiators were not careful about the important contents of the treaty (Declaration of Algiers) but they were careful that the document is called "declaration" so that the political players at home do not blame them for making a "treaty" with the Americans. Some experts have called this "declaration" (treaty) as something worse than the imposed treaties of Golestan and Turkamanchai that resulted in separation of parts of the Iranian Azerbaijan and annexation of them to the Russia in the Qajar period (end of the nineteenth century). On the basis of this declaration (treaty) one of the most bizarre creatures in the history of the international arbitration tribunals was created. The Iranian policy makers waited so long that the ICJ in fact condemned Iran for violation of the Vienna Conventions on the Diplomatic and Consular Relations, and Iran lost many other options. The Americans who had in fact showed some kind of sympathy to the new regime of Iran (some people think that the Americans brought the Mullahs to power to help the policy of containment against the communist USSR, through the Green Belt), started to think of opposing the regime (according to some reports they persuaded Saddam to attack Iran).

In the early stages of the hostage crisis, there were hundreds of solutions proposed by the Americans and third parties to solve the case, and the regime rejected all of them. In this case, the negotiators were more concerned about the people behind them as compared to the people in front of them.

In the case of Iran-Iraq war, again we see a pattern of prolonging the case until the worst option is imposed. In various stages of the war, there were so many proposals by the United Nations, Non-aligned Movement, various international organizations, Arab countries, Arab League, and individuals of international importance for solving the problem and stopping two countries from killing each other in one of the bloodiest wars in human history.

After taking back Khoramshahr from the forces of Saddam, the Arab countries, especially Saudi Arabia and Kuwait were ready to pay good money to Iran as compensation for war damages and end the hostilities. Khomeini rejected it. The regime of Iran did not accept any of the proposals until it was forced to accept the 598 Resolution of the United Nations Security Council. The rejection of the existing solutions and proposals continued until Saddam completed its arsenal of chemical weapons. At the end of war in 1988, the Iraqis were killing the Iranian soldiers the way one would kill ants with pesticides.

The military strategy of "human waves" no longer worked against chemical weapons. The Iranian army lost the control over the territories that it had gained in Iraq and the Iranian forces immediately and without any order retreated. At the same time, the Americans destroyed more half of the Iranian navy in a couple of hours. Khomeini thought there was no way to save the regime but to end the war which he called "drinking from the chalice of poison".

He stepped on his own words and claims about the divine duty to fight Saddam and before the eyes of the astonished people of Iran, he chose to live and forget about martyrdom. I think this was the second time that he was resorting to the diplomacy of drinking the chalice of poison.

The reality is that Iran had not intended to accept Resolution 598, nor was there genuine interest in resolving the issues that divided the two sides. The Security Council had adopted 598 a year earlier, in 1987. What changed Iran's position was not proposals of the Iranian military and political strategists (who were in fact a group of naive ideologues unschooled in political geography, international relations and power politics). There was one, and only one, reason for acceptance of the peace: the regime of the Islamic Republic was in danger of collapse in the face of decisive defeats on the battlefield and poor morale within military ranks and among the populace.

What ultimately drove the Iranian regime to accept 598 was fear that the regime would fall. As far as the Iraqis were concerned, from their new position of strength, they had no wish either to settle for peace or to abide by their acceptance of 598, which had come a year earlier, almost immediately after its adoption by the Security Council. Saddam argued that facts on the ground had now changed - the Iranians having been pushed out of Iraqi territory - and he had no interest in accepting the peace. What stopped the Iraqis was pressure from the West, especially the U.S. By then, the U.S. was on fairly good terms with Saddam and he went along and accepted Resolution 598.

The approach of the Iranian regime was generally:

1- Continuation of the negotiations as long as possible in the hope that something good happens (especially due to religious arrogance)

2- Refraining from giving a clear answer to the proposals for solution

3- Showing generally that the existing proposals are too little for solving the problem and the other side must be ready for giving big advantages (in the case of the hostages, giving the Shah back to Iran, and in the case of the Iran-Iraq war, ousting of Saddam and Ba'ath party in Iraq)

4- Accept the last possible proposal after putting the regime in the situation that it faces collapse

5- Accepting the last though the worst solution as compared with the previous options

In the case of the 2003 proposals of the Iranian regime (the proposal apparently delivered by the Iranian regime to the US for solving their problems in general), it is important to note that at that time the US had attacked the Iraqi regime's army. The regime of Iran watched with great concern how Saddam's huge army was crushed in a couple of days. They thought the regime of Iran was next. The US ignored the Iranian proposals because there was a strong feeling in the US that the other trouble makers in the region would be eliminated one by one.

In light of Iran's track record when it comes to negotiating in the above cases and looking at the behaviors of the Iranian negotiators (especially noting that the government of Iran, headed by

President Ahmadinejad, keeps saying that they are determined to go back to the time of Khomeini and do as he did) one can expect the same result in IRI's third important case of negotiation, i.e. the nuclear case of Iran. In other words, the Iranian regime will only stop its present nuclear policy when the regime is made to appreciate that it is about to collapse.

The big question is: does the regime feel that it has to drink the chalice of poison now? The answer is no. The reasons are:

A- The regime in Iran believes it is still stable.

B- They have learned how to live without the US. They want important advantages from the US.

C- The Western states (especially the members of the 5+1 Group) have different approaches to the government of Iran and its nuclear program. The Chinese have made it clear that they do not want any serious sanctions against Iran. The Russians are the main source of encouragement for the regime of Tehran. They have many interests in the economic and political relations with Iran and enjoy bilaterally and multilaterally from the bad US-Iran relations, (in relations with Iran and in relations with the US). The EU members are more afraid of the US than Iran.

D- Iran believes that the US is not ready to go for a military option due to the situation in Iraq, Lebanon, and Afghanistan.

E- The Iranian government is in deep trouble inside the country. People are dissatisfied, the economy is bad, and people are unemployed. Crisis is good for the Iranian government. After all, Khomeini, the so-called founder of the Islamic Republic in Iran used to call the war with Iraq (1980-1988) a God given gift for the ruling system. The government of Iran welcomes crisis.

F- Sanctions alone do not stop Iran from trying to achieve its nuclear ambitions. The Iranian regime has experience in violating sanctions as a result of dealing with Iraq and helping Iraq get around sanctions when Iraq was under UN sanctions.

G- The Islamic regime in Iran is a troubled system. It has failed in economic, political, social and even cultural fields and it constantly blames the US for all of its problems. Good US-Iran relations while they may be good for the Iranian people, is not good for the regime because it will no longer have a scapegoat.

H- The regime of Iran considers the US as personification of all values that the regime opposes. For the same reason, what it will gain from relations with the US must be so important to compensate for such a great loss. The regime needs to defend its policies, suppress the people, violate human rights, close the newspapers and kill the opponents. Is the USA ready to give the regime of Iran these concessions? These concessions are against everything the US stands for and as such it does not seem that the US will be bowing down to Iran on these points and the regime of Iran knows that very well.

I- The regime of Iran feels that it has a divine mission to change the world order. The followers of the Hidden Imam in Iran think that he is going to appear and conquer the whole world and they should make themselves ready for the war in the army of the Hidden Imam. The regime of the Islamic Republic of Iran believes that it has a divine duty to fight the Western culture and impose policies that it considers to be Islamic. The regime of the Islamic Republic of Iran believes in the supremacy of the version of Islam practiced by the Iranian Mullahs as the best arrangement for the whole world and it follows that such a system cannot have a genuine intention for living in peace with the West.

J- The regime of the Islamic Republic of Iran believes that the Western way of life is corrupt and the Western democracies are going to fall, as the USSR fell. It does not believe in validity of any arrangement with the "Western" infidels and all of the agreements with the West are temporary and subject to abrogation as soon as the Islamic power has the opportunity to do so.

K- When Ahmadinejad proposed to talk to the US president and later when he wrote several letters to the Western leaders, including the US president, there was strong understanding that he was only trying to make a public relations stunt to show support for popular topics such as respecting justice, humanity and religions, especially Islam. For the same reason, the Western leaders chose not to respond to the letters. Nothing has changed as far as the world leaders are concerned. They still convinced that Iran uses opportunities such as letter writing as propaganda and not real attempt to talk about controversial issues.

L- The Iranian officials have come to the conclusion that the proposal such as establishment of the Visa Office in Tehran is impractical for the US. While the US government is accused of all plots to topple the regime of Iran and Iran believes that the US officials have approved a budget for this purpose and places like VOA and Radio Farda are accused of trying to destabilize the population of Iran through their programs, how is it possible to have an office of the Americans in Tehran? Who guarantees their safety and security and even if some Iranian officials would do that, what value can the US attach to such a guarantee? The government of Iran is still not ready to call the hostage taking in 1979 in the US embassy in Tehran as a wrongful act. Many of the Hostage takers are still in the government (although some of them have turned to reformists, the majority of them are still in the government, including Ahmadinejad). The government of the Islamic Republic in Tehran has proved time and again that it has no respect for the welfare of the people, especially if it is in contrast with the security of the regime.

WHAT IRAN IS LOSING TO GET NUCLEAR ENERGY?

How much have Iranians paid and will pay to have nuclear electricity can be seen in many aspects of the Iranian life:

Economy

a- Oil: Iranian economy depends on oil exports. However, Iran's oil industry is a house of cards. It is neglected, crumbling and underinvested. Many of its oil and gas fields are in dire need of foreign technical expertise.

b- Gas: While holding the second largest natural gas reserves in the world, Iran is not a serious exporter of the commodity. The EU seeks a lowering of its dependence on Russian energy, and Iran potentially could benefit by joining projects like the Nabucco gas pipeline. However, Iran's isolation and its poor relations with the international community are impediments. The so-called peace pipeline between Iran, Pakistan and India has not made any progress in spite of the enormous price reductions proposed by Iran. Iran's single most important source of natural gas is the South Pars field in the Persian Gulf which Iran holds in common with Qatar. The tiny emirate across the Persian Gulf has been exploiting gas from South Pars to the tune of billions of dollars, while Iranians helplessly witness the depletion of the reserves.

c- Iranian politicians have claimed many times that Iran's international isolation and the economic sanctions—including those imposed by the UN Security Council—have not hurt the country seriously, and they insist on continuing the nuclear program at all costs. In reality, however, Iran's oil and gas industry have suffered and will suffer further.

d- Pipelines and transit: The projected construction of oil and gas pipelines over the next 25 to 50 years all bypass Iranian territory and Iran will lose the transit fees, jobs, investment and prestige that accompany such projects. The United States supports Nabucco as a way of avoiding Russian participation in the European gas-supply chain, and has backed the participation of Azerbaijan, Kazakhstan, and especially Turkmenistan in the project. Brussels and Washington are supporting the construction of a Trans-Caspian natural-gas pipeline to run from either Kazakhstan, or more likely from Turkmenistan, along the seabed to Azerbaijan, where the gas would be pumped into pipelines leading to Nabucco.

e- Investment in other sectors: Iran's mineral wealth, in addition to oil and gas, includes chromites, lead, zinc, copper, coal, gold, tin, iron, manganese, ferrous oxide, and tungsten. Commercial extraction of significant reserves of turquoise, fireclay, and kaolin is also possible. Prior to the Revolution in 1979, the government intended to develop the copper industry to the point that it would rival oil as a source of foreign exchange. Iranian copper deposits are among the world's largest. These sectors suffer from lack of technology and investment.

f- Tourism: According to the World Ecotourism Organization, Iran is a country with high tourism potential and attractions. Iran, which ranks seventh worldwide in terms of tourist attractions, can earn billions from tourism. As a country with rich civilization and history, Iran unfortunately has a tiny share in the global tourist revenue. Countries like Turkey and Spain are making the equivalent of Iran's oil revenue from tourism.

E- Failure to acquire World Trade Organization membership and inability to perform banking operations at the international level.

F- Being forced to buy many things on the black market at higher prices and without proper inspections' procedures.

G- The Iranian civilian airlines are in shambles. Iran has been forced to resort to the black market to gain even the second hand aircraft. The Russians and Chinese have sold many substandard airplanes to Iran and the government and people of Iran are really dissatisfied with these.

H- Getting loans from international institutions have faced difficulties.

1- Being deprived of the assistance that the IAEA provides to the states for their nuclear activities under the IAEA's rules.

2- Political issues

a- Bad relations with many states, including the US is depriving the Iranian nation of many benefits if interaction with these countries. The Russians and the Chinese and some other countries are getting advantages both from Iran and the West due to the situation of Iran. The conditions in the Caspian Sea, the treatment of Russians in the Bushehr Power Plant, and sale of outdated items, including all kinds of the military equipment to Iran are only some examples.

b- Loss of international prestige. This has caused Iran to lose in many fields including cultural affairs, scientific issues, membership and activity in many international forums and organizations including the UN and its numerous specialized agencies, OPEC, and even regional organizations.

c- If the confrontation on the nuclear issue leads to military operations in various levels (such as the US and Israeli attack on the nuclear installations, or the US and Israeli attack on the entire infrastructure of Iran), the destruction and possible disintegration of Iran will be the ultimate cost that Iranians will pay.

These points beg the question how much must the people of Iran pay for nuclear electricity under present conditions and why not accept complete transparency in the program claimed to be peaceful?

WHO ARE BAHA'IS AND WHY THE REGIME OF IRAN HATES THEM?

Recently, the United States Department of State has criticized the Iranian regime for restricting religious freedom. "...There was a further deterioration of the extremely poor status of respect for religious freedom during the reporting period, most notably for Baha'is and Sufi Muslims. ... There were reports of imprisonment, harassment, intimidation, and discrimination based on religious beliefs", the State Department said in its annual International Religious Freedom Report 2006. The report said that Iran's theocratic government had created a "threatening atmosphere" for nearly all religious minorities". It chastised Tehran's "harsh and oppressive" treatment of religious minorities. Since 1999, the Secretary of State has designated Iran as a "Country of Particular Concern" under the International Religious Freedom Act for particularly severe violations of religious freedom.(1)

On 16 of December 2005, the United Nations General assembly adopted a resolution about serious violation of human rights in the Islamic Republic of Iran which included a reference to violation of the rights of the religious and ethnic minorities, such as Bahai's in Iran. (2)

The questions that arise are: Who are the Baha'is? What do they think and why does the Iranian regime hate them?

According to wikipedia: "The Bahá'í Faith is a religion founded by Bahaullah in 19th century Persia. Bahá'ís number around 6 million in more than 200 countries around the world. According to Bahá'í teachings, religious history is seen as an evolving educational process for mankind, through God's messengers, which are termed Manifestations of God. Bahaullah is seen as the most recent, pivotal, but not final of these individuals. He claimed to be the long-expected educator and teacher of all peoples, prophesied in Christianity, Islam, Hinduism, Buddism and other religions, and that his mission was to establish a firm basis for unity throughout the world, and inaugurate an age of peace and justice, which Bahá'ís expect will inevitably arise".(3)

The same source says, "Bahá'ís regard the period from the Bab's 1844 declaration in Shiraz, to the 1921 passing of Abdul-Baha [Bahaullah's son], as the Heroic Age of the Faith. During this period its early believers experienced great persecution and its foundations were established in several countries around the world. The period after 1921 is described as the Formative Age. Shoghi Effendi characterized this era as coinciding with the Bahá'í Faith's emergence from obscurity, by the establishment and "maturation" of its administrative institutions, and by the faith's world-wide expansion. He indicated that the Formative Age would eventually transition into a future Golden Age in which the Bahá'í Faith "is embraced by the majority of the peoples of a number of the Sovereign States of the world".(4)

Although since the old times the Bahai's faced hardships and persecutions in Iran and other Islamic countries, and an unknown number of them have been killed, prosecuted and discriminated against in those countries, since the beginning of the so-called Islamic Revolution in Iran, a kind of official anti-Bahai policy is followed by the regime. In fact, some of the prominent figures of the Islamic regime of Iran were among the members of the notorious "Counter-Bahai Associations" in Iran. "... over 200 [Baha'i] believers were executed between 1978 and 1998. Since the Islamic Revolution of 1979, Iranian Bahá'ís have regularly had their homes ransacked or been banned from attending university or holding government jobs, and several hundred have received prison sentences for their religious beliefs, most recently for participating in study circles. Bahá'í cemeteries have been desecrated and property seized and occasionally demolished, including the House of Mírzá Burzurg, Bahá'u'lláh's father. The House of the Báb in Shiraz has been destroyed twice, and is one of three sites to which Bahá'ís perform pilgrimage." (5)

Even more recently the situation of Bahá'ís has worsened; the United Nations Commission on Human Rights revealed an October 2005 confidential letter from Command Headquarters of the Armed Forces of Iran to identify Bahá'ís and to monitor their activities and in November 2005 the state-run and influential Kayhan newspaper, whose managing editor is appointed by Iran's supreme leader, Ayatollah Khamenei ran nearly three dozen articles defaming the Bahá'í Faith.

Due to these actions, the Special Rapporteur of the United Nations Commission on Human Rights stated on March 20, 2006 that she "also expresses concern that the information gained as a result of such monitoring will be used as a basis for the increased persecution of, and discrimination against, members of the Bahá'í faith, in violation of international standards. ... The Special Rapporteur is concerned that this latest development indicates that the situation with regard to religious minorities in Iran is, in fact, deteriorating." (6)

"Some 300,000 Baha'is live throughout Iran, making the Baha'i Faith the country's largest minority religion. Baha'is have been targets of discrimination and violence in Iran since the religion began there in the mid-nineteenth century...Today the Iranian government regards Baha'is as apostates and unprotected infidels. Baha'is in Iran have no legal rights, and they are not permitted to elect leaders of their community....Baha'is in Iran are systematically denied jobs, pensions and the right to inherit property. More than 10,000 Baha'is have been dismissed from government and university posts since Iran's 1979 revolution. Consistent with the Supreme Revolutionary Cultural Council's 1991 memorandum, Baha'i youth in Iran have been barred from higher education for more than 25 years. (7)

The officials of the Islamic regime of Iran and the members of the anti-Baha'i groups in Iran have long accused the Bahai's of distorting the religion of Islam. Also, they have claimed that Bahai's have acted as the tools of the foreign powers in Iran. Of course, as far as the first accusation is concerned, Shiites are themselves under attack by the majority of Muslims who are Sunnis of doing the same thing. Many Sunnis do not accept Shiites as the followers of Islam at all.

Regarding the second one, apparently the government cannot make up its mind as to which foreign government "established" the Bahai Faith because the Bahai's have been accused of being created by the British, the Americans and even the Russians in Iran. The real reason of the hostility of the Islamic governments, especially the Iranian regime, towards the Baha'is, is explained by Bernard Lewis, the famous Philosopher, who has said, "...the Muslim piety and Islamic authorities have always had great difficulty in accommodating post-Islamic monotheistic religions such as Baha'is... [whose]their very existence presents a challenge to the Islamic doctrine of the perfection and finality of Muhammad's revelation. (8)

Also, in the same context, a report by the US Department of State in 2004 states: "Baha'is were considered apostates because of their claim to a religious revelation subsequent to that of the Prophet Mohammed. The Government defined the Baha'i Faith as a political sect linked to the Pahlavi monarchy and therefore, as counter-revolutionary. Historically at risk, Baha'is often have suffered increased levels of mistreatment during times of political unrest. Baha'is may not teach or practice their faith or maintain links with co-religionists abroad. The Government continued to imprison and detain Baha'is based on their religious beliefs. A 2001 Ministry of Justice report indicated that government policy aimed at the eventual elimination of the Baha'is as a community." (9)

It is interesting to note that the Shiites have generally the same situation in the Islamic world that Bahai's have in the Islamic regime of Iran. The ideological Islamic regime is hostage to certain principles that it considers to be true interpretation of

Islam. This interpretation is only one of the many interpretations of Islam (that can differ from ultra right to the ultra left in the political spectrum) and a great number of the supporters of other interpretations do not approve of or even hate the Shiites.

It is true that the Islamic regime of Iran has a special hatred towards Bahai's. However, this hatred precedes the present regime of Iran. It is not really important whether the claims of Bahai's about the origin of their religion and their interpretation of historical events are right or wrong. They have the same rights as others to practice their own beliefs. Treatment of the Bahai's by the Iranian regime and all those who have harassed the Bahai's in Iran due to their religious convictions has always been a violation of human rights and should be condemned as such. Those Iranians who feel a kind of baseless hostility towards the Bahai's and those who think that Bahai's are a disgrace to the Shiite Islam, should pause and ponder the situation of Shiites in the Islamic world given that 90% of the Muslims (Sunnis) think of the Shiites the same way.

The people of Iran should know that "Bahai killings" (killing men, women and children of Bahai's), under the guidance and religious orders of the Mullahs of Iran, as a kind of silent genocide, was one of the darkest chapters of the Iranian history. The Iranians should condemn such heinous crimes and express their regrets and get ready to apologize.

(1) http://www.iranifocus.com/modules/news/print.php?storyid= 8654, dated 09/16/06

(2) Persian Journal, Human Rights in Iran, Contradiction of the Universal Standards with the dominant ideology, dated 12/19/2005

(3) Baha'i Faith, the Wikipedia http://en.wikipedia.org/wiki/ Bah%C3%A1%C3%ADf Faith.

(4) Baha'i Faith, the Wikipedia http://en.wikipedia.org/wiki/ Bah%C3%A1%C3%ADf Faith.

(5) http://www.bahai.us/persecution-bahais-iran.

(6) Baha'i Faith, the Wikipedia http://en.wikipedia.org/wiki/Bah%C3%A1%C3%ADf Faith.

(7) http://www.bahai.us/persecution-bahais-iran.

(8) Baha'i Faith, the Wikipedia http://en.wikipedia.org/wiki/Bah%C3%A1%C3%ADf Faith

(9) Report of the US Depatment of State in 2004, the Country Reports onn the Human Rights Practices, Released by the Bureau of Democracxy, Human Righrts, and Labor, 25 Feb. 2004.

What is Wrong with the Islamic Republic of Iran?

The regime of the Islamic Republic of Iran has many problems. Some of them are inherent and they come from the very institution of the "Islamic Republic", as two words that do not go together. Some others are due to the characteristics of the Iranian rulers. The most important problems of the present regime of Iran are:

The contradictions of the political system

The Islamic Republic of Iran has not yet decided that it wants to be a revolutionary movement or a responsible state in the international system. The foreign policy of Iran, as defined by the constitutional laws and the practices of the Iranian regime, indicate to conflicting points in this field. At the same time, the political system of Iran is based on an unknown and vague concept that is hazily prepared to fit the government of the religious leaders.

Some politicians in the Islamic Republic of Iran claim what today exists in Iran (or what should exist) is a "religious democracy". The question is: can democracy be religious or this expression is per se an oxymoron. The religious limitations have always been the greatest enemy of the liberty, human rights and democracy.

What exists in Iran is an Islamic-Shiite theocracy based on the new concept of Valie-Faghigh (Government of the religious experts). The latter is a fabrication of the modem Islamic theo-reticians and it has no roots in any part of Islamic history. Just like the expression of "Ayatollah" (Sign of God) which is less than a few decades old and it was born during the Constitutional Rev-olution in Iran, the government of a supreme Islamic leader is completely rootless. (For a comprehensive study about the roots of expressions like "Ayatollah" please refer to the article of Jalal Maini, "Spiritual Titles in Iranian Shitism", in Persian, with an abstract in English, Iran Nameh, Persian Periodical, Foundation for Iranian Studies, Vol. 1, No.4, Summer 1983, Washington DC).

At the same time, this product has failed to answer any prob-lem of the Islamic societies. What has happened in Iran during the last thirty years has demonstrated that the concept of Valie-faghih is a dysfunctional and even dangerous idea, comparable to the inquisition in the Medieval Europe.

Lack of secularism

The experience of Islamic revolution in Iran proved once again that mixture of politics and Islam, in the world, which is divided into nation-states and the governments, which are designed to follow the national interests, does not work. The Iranian experi-ence had a great deal of impact on many Muslim countries. The tide of Islamic revolutions in all these countries has died. The Islamic revolution should have happened in countries like Egypt and Algeria much sooner than Iran, but the experience of Iranian "Islamic" revolution stopped them. No great Islamic revolution is in the making. On the other hand, many people in all Islamic societies are trying to separate their religion from politics. What is happening in Iran at the present juncture is a clear struggle by the people of Iran to get religion separated from politics.

Acting as "revolutionary"

Revolutionary is used as a respected word in the IR of Iran, but in reality after 30 years of the "revolution" whoever is called revo-lutionary is in fact a corrupt and crook person.

In the early years of any revolution, the officials of the new regime, try to control the affairs through "revolutionary" methods and by "revolutionary persons" because they want to do many things in a short period of time and they feel that if they want to observe all the standards or legal or even customary and logical process of doing things, they may lose the main game. Therefore, "revolutionary" acts are a kind of temporary and limited actions taken by the new regime until the affairs return to their conditions, and they go back to observe logic, standards, due processes, laws and so on. It is not acceptable that a regime like the Islamic Republic of Iran, after a quarter century of dominance over the country still they speak of revolutionary persons, institutions, practices and so on.

Therefore, the expression of "revolutionary" in Iran is a reference to violation of laws and standards and due process. The Islamic revolutionary courts that were established in the early years of the so-called Islamic revolution were aimed at rapid trial of the persons that the new regime considered as the enemies. These courts condemned thousands of people to death, without observing any laws. They have claimed in various occasions that they enforce the Islamic codes. However, in reality they have only enforced the views of the ruling circles disguised as Islamic codes. It is notable that starting from the first Islamic revolutionary courts up to now, no prominent Islamic clergy has accepted to be a judge or a high-ranking official in the Islamic Revolutionary courts. These courts are full of the young and ambitious clergies that they have their positions and promotions only due to the obedience to the ruling circles. These courts claim to be "revolutionary" in the sense that they do have the time and patience of observing the existing laws and legal procedures. They take their decisions on odd sources like the "personal view of the Islamic Judge", the religious rulings of the important sources of the Taqleed (imitation) in the Shiite-Islamic society, and especially the Resaleh (book of the Islamic rulings) of Ayatollah Khomeini. This means that a judge may condoms a person to death with reference to a certain page of the Resaleh of Ayatollah Khomeini.

Although this practice was unacceptable even in the early years of the "revolution" (due to contradiction to the Universal Declaration of the Hunan Rights, the International Convention on the Civil and Political Rights, and the International Convention on the Social and Economic Rights, that all of them are ratified by Iran and even without ratification, they are part of the laws in force for all states in the world), After 30 years of the so-called revolution, what is the use of such courts? The "revolutionary" courts are per se violation of the due processes of implementation and enforcing laws and they are a symbol of "lawlessness", and double standard. How is it possible to have two legal systems in one country? This legal chaos has not only violated the rights of the Iranian citizens, they have been the source of the reluctance of the foreign sources for tackling (or investing) in Iran? The foreign companies that are active in Iran have in fact concluded agreements with the government that takes the possible conflicts of the two sides out of the jurisdiction of the Iranian courts and make them dependent on international arbitrations and other forms of the international litigation. In order to reform the system, the revolutionary courts must be eliminated and many of the cases that they have tried must be retried according to the laws and legal procedures.

The institutions, such the Bonyade Mostazafan (the Foundation for the Deprived), Bonyade 15th of Khordad, the Charity Foundation of Imam Khomieni, and countless other institutions that are collectively called "revolutionary institutions" are in fact center for the activity of the ruling circles in the Islamic Republic of Iran, without observing the laws of the land or as a matter of fact any law.

These institutions give loans to the sheepish followers of the regime, pay huge amounts of money to the clergies, send money for the terrorist organizations in various countries, organize and operate their own systems of accounting (they do not pay taxes), they have their own ports of importation and exportation without paying the due taxes to customs officials of get inspected by the legal authorities, they recruit thousands of people without observing the national laws, they send students to the universities without passing the difficult entrance examination of the Iranian universities, they buy , sell, and produce whatever they wish without observing the regulations or getting permits and licenses and so on. In short, the "revolutionary" institutions in the Islamic Republic of Iran are the center for corruption and complexes of the organized criminal activities.

"Revolutionary" persons are considered as qualified persons for all positions in the Islamic Republic of Iran. Whenever, there is a discussion in the Majles, media, government and so on, they are "looking for revolutionary persons for the jobs". However, revolutionary persons at the moment are the most unqualified persons for any post. "Revolutionary persons", as the people who do not observe laws, do not get proper consultation, impose their own views as if they are the single most important point reference for any issue (usually without having the least required standards), and do not care about the criticisms (even if they have a justified point) are the worst choice for any job. In fact, most the "revolutionary" managers of the Islamic Republic of Iran must stand a trial for their illegal actions.

All those who speak about returning to the earlier years of the Islamic revolution (including and especially the "revolutionary" president of Iran), mean they do not want to observe even what they have set as laws. They want to be free to take any action that they desire under the pretext of being revolutionary. In a nutshell, any person that calls himself "revolutionary" in the present regime of Iran is in fact "counter-revolutionary" even by the standards of the current regime.

The Green Movement of Iran

The Green Movement of Iran emerged during and after the presidential elections in Iran. The rival of Mahmoud Ahmadinejad, Mir Hussein Mousavi and his supporters had chosen the green for their campaign due to the relations of this color with Islam (the Flag of Islamic forces was green in the history) and also peacefulness of the notion. However, unlike the claims of many persons, including some of the known leaders of the movement, the notion had strong connection with the colored movements or velvet revolutions of the other countries. The supporters of the Green Movement of Iran, tried seriously, and are still trying to use the same methods of the velvet revolutions, especially color wise.

After the elections and victory of Ahmadinejad to gain the presidency, the supporters of Mousavi, joined by some other groups objected to the results is a wave of resistance which is called Green Movement. Therefore, the Green Movement of Iran has nothing to do with the Green Movements, especially in the Western countries for protection of the environment and stopping the negative effects of human activities on the climate. For the same reason, the supporters and leaders of the Greens in Iran have no real objection to the nuclear program of Iran and even immediately after the Geneva Accords of Iran and the 5+1 for a kind of exchange of the enriched materials, one of the persons who spoke against it was no one other than the Mir Hussein Mousavi.

Although a round of rigged elections led to renewing Ahmadinejad's tenure as the president of the Islamic Republic of Iran. However, this was nothing new. There have never been democratic elections in Iran after the so called Islamic Revolution in 1979 (or as matter of fact, even before that). However, the new element was the mass protests of the people and a part of the regime to the results of the recent elections.

The entire system of the Islamic Republic has been based on shame elections and people like the leaders of the Green Movement of Iran had important posts in Iran due to and using the same corrupt system. Therefore it was not the ruling regime of Iran who changed the rules of the game in the middle of the game, it was the leaders of the movement to replace Ahmadinejad with Mir Hussein Mousavi who took advantage of the people's Green Movement and tried to use it for their own aims.

Combination of Supporters and leaders

This divide in the demands of the Green Movement and the so called leaders of the movement in Iran still exists. These leaders are apparently Mir Huesin Mousavi (former PM) , Karroubi (Former Speaker of the Parliament) , Mohammad Khatami (former president), and up to a limit, Hashemi Rafsanjani (Head of the Expediency Council). These leaders are religious figures with strong reliance and trust to the Islamic regime and its supreme leaders especially Ayatollah Khomeini. However, a look at the people who were demonstrating in the street, the people who were arrested as the organizers of the movement and people who are under attack from the regime reveals that most of them are younger generations of Iran fed up with the Islamic regime, along with the reformists and a group of opportunists Islamic elements who just want to see a change of administration. Neda Agha Sultan, the most well known image of this movement, was an Iranian girl without the traditional Islamic look (clothes, make up and covering the head ...), who was going to the "music class" (very un-Islamic), along with her music teacher (if a girl is stopped in a street of Tehran, while walking or even is a car, by the disciplinary forces [police] and she is asked "who is the man with you?" and she answers "my music teacher". She can be arrested immediately, along with her "music teacher").

What I am trying to say is that the Green Movement of Iran was formed and it is still going on, by various elements who in general wanted to move Iran in the direction of democracy, freedom, human rights, advancement, and against religious fanatics, rule of the outdated laws of religion, welfare of the people, stopping Iran from meddling in other affairs and similar issues. At the same time, the so-called leaders, such those that I mentioned, have never intended to move in such directions, because they know this line leads to the collapse of a regime that has made them present figures and they will go down along with all others in the regime.

Review of the Hostage-Taking at the American Embassy in Iran

On 4th of November 1979 a group who called themselves the "Students Following the Line of Imam" took over the American Embassy in Tehran and took 52 diplomats hostage and kept them for 444 days.

Attacking foreign diplomats and embassies by an angry and spontaneously-formed group of people was not unprecedented in the history of Iran and other countries. In 1829, following the Turkamanchi Treaty that separated some parts of Iran and annexed them to Russia under imposed conditions, a group of agitated Iranians attacked the Russian embassy and killed all of the staff, including the Russian ambassador, Alexander Griboyedov. (1)

What made the 1979 attack against the American Embassy different from the other incidents was that Ayatollah R. Khomieni, the Supreme Leader of Iran at that time, supported this move and turned the action against American Embassy into a national and governmental issue and a matter of state responsibility.

Most of the persons that formed the so-called students following the line of Imam that took over the American Embassy in Tehran were not students. They were active members or sympathizers of the MKOs, the Leftist Marxist-Leninist Group of Fadaian Khalgh, and the Communist Tudeh party of Iran. (2)

R. K. Ramazani, in his article about the Iran's Hostage Crisis, writes: "...The Islamist students who took over the American Embassy claimed to follow the Khomeini line (Khatt-i Imam),.... the dominant ideology that influenced the students' action is difficult to identify. Massoumeh Ebtekar, the revolutionary students' spokesperson, claims that they were influenced by Ali Shariati, who, she says, persuaded them to accept the leadership of Imam Khomeini with courage and devotion.' I have not been able to verify this statement." (3)

Mehdi Salimi, writing in Persian for Baztab website (4), has said: "Four hundred students and the people, who were marching towards the Tehran University since ten o'clock in the morning to protest the US policies, suddenly changed their course and entered the American Embassy. They took 72 persons out of the embassy staff as hostage and captured the embassy. This was in fact the second time since the victory of the Iranian Islamic Revolution in 1979 that the American Embassy in Tehran was taken over.

In February of the same year, almost 150 persons who belonged to the leftist forces and a group called Cherikhaye Fadaian Khalgh, who were convinced that the documents of SAVAK [Shah's secret police] had been transferred to the American Embassy, and who were provoked by articles appearing in a newspaper in Baku [the Capital of Azerbaijan Republic, which was then still a part of the USSR], attacked the American Embassy. This incident was settled by good offices of figures such as Martyr Beheshti." (5)

During the 14 months that the crisis lasted, the so-called students published numerous books about the documents that they had apparently found in the American Embassy (including what they had retrieved from the documents shredded in the shredding machines). However, not a single page of those documents contained anything about the mullahs that had gained power in Iran. On the other side, they did everything possible to demonstrate that the Americans were in touch with certain persons to change the course of the revolution and act against the interests of the people of Iran.

It was a known fact in those days (and it has been proved many times since then) that the prominent mullahs, including Khomeini, personally and directly were in touch with the American officials before and after the Islamic Revolution in Iran in 1979. However, the so-called students who published 53 volumes of books about the documents of the former American Embassy (they called it "Den of Spies"), never published a single sentence referring to any of these contacts.

The hostage-taking crisis in the American Embassy in Tehran was an act against the standards of international law, Iran's national interests of Iran and even against the principles of Iranians themselves. The incident of hostage taking at the American Embassy cost the government and people of Iran dearly. Some of the problems created for Iran due to this incident were as follows:

a- Isolation of Iran in the international community

b- The loss of possible positive reaction of the US officials towards the new regime. (6)

c- Stopping of the Iran-US relations

d- Start of an artificial stage in the US-Iran relations. On one side, the government of the Islamic Republic insisted on the hostility towards the USA, and on the other side, the people of Iran loved the USA.

e- Gradual inclination of the USA to confront the regime of Iran

f- Creation of a wall of distrust between two states

g- Comparative support of the Iraqis in the Iran-Iraq war (1980-88)

h- Discrediting Iran in international forums like the UNSC and ICJ (it condemned Iran for violation of the Vienna Conventions on Diplomatic and Consular Relations).

John Limbert, a former American hostage in Tehran and a political figure in the embassy in 1979, who had to spend nine months in solitary confinement, has said, "What they did to their country and society was much worse than what they did to us.

They helped today's ruling clique gain their grip on power. They helped to ensure that mob rule and chants of the goon squad triumphed." (7)

It is clear from many sources, including the book published by Massomeh Ebtekar that the students were acting in a professional and pre-planned way. Talking to ISNA on the occasion of the anniversary of the Embassy Take over, Ebtekar has said, "... the students had reached the conclusion that they have to do something very big that gets tremendous attention... the group of 300 to 400 persons attacked the embassy. Some students climbed the walls. The women had hidden big pliers under their Islamic veil and used them to cut the chains of the gates. The students were very concerned to stop the ordinary people from entering the embassy...." (8)

Ebtekar, who was known as "Mary' to the journalists that covered the incident and translated the documents for the hostage takers, has tried in her book (9) to give the impression that she was not a member of the hostage takers.

In fact, she was a hostage taker. Her husband (Hashemi) was also one of the hostage takers. She was rewarded for her role in this incident later by receiving a scholarship from the Iranian government to get PhD from a Western university and became the Deputy President and Head of the Iranian Environment Protection Organization. Some of the other so-called students of the line of Imam were rewarded later by becoming prominent officials in the Iranian oil ministry.

Also a number of them became high ranking officials and ambassadors of the Iranian foreign ministry. Shiekholislam, who was a long time Deputy Foreign Minister of Iran in Political affairs, during the tenure of Dr. Velayati, was one of the leaders of the so-called students. Another leader of the so-called students was Mohsen Mirdamadi, who later became a prominent member of the Iranian Intelligence Ministry. Also Saeed Hajjarian, Ibrahim Asgharzadeh and Abbas Abdi gained many positions in the government due to their criminal acts against the national interest of Iran.

The takeover of the embassy was not an instantaneous act at all. The criminals who did this had planned everything before. They had communication devices that belonged to the law enforcement officials and they were armed. The attackers were well aware (probably by listening to the telephone calls of the American Embassy) that the charge d'affaires and two other officials of the American Embassy were out of the embassy and they were waiting for them to return. Eventually, when it was clear that the three diplomats were not returning soon, they went ahead and attacked the embassy.

Khomeini had provoked the people to act against the USA, but he did not know about the plan to attack the American Embassy. First, he asked his foreign minister, Dr. Ebrahim Yazdi (according to the interviews of Yazdi with the Iranian media on the occasion of the anniversary of the embassy takeover), to go and throw out the students, but later the students (and the leftist agents) convinced Khomeini that he could use the existing documents (or documents that did not exist, but he could claim that they have it) to discredit his opponents. Khomeini, who was a master manipulator (the clerics stole the Iranian revolution which belonged to all Iranians and was not supposed to be a religious movement), rode the wave and accepted to support the move, without considering Iran's national interests.

Some of the documents that were used by the so-called students to discredit the target persons were ridiculous. In one case (the case of Engineer Abbas Amir Entezam, the Spokesperson of the Interim Government of Iran, who was later arrested and put in prison for espionage and he is still there after 30 years), the students showed a letter to Khomeini from the American Embassy addressed to Amir Entezam that has started with "Dear Sir" and they argued that Amir Entezam was so close to the Americans that they called him "Dear Sir".

It is interesting that years later, when some of the so-called Students of the Line of Imam started to act a little different from the official line (some of them supported the relations with the USA, some said that they regretted that they were part of this action and others appeared as supporters of reforms), they were tried and imprisoned by the same ridiculous methods and absurd criteria. Abbas Abdi, one of the leading hostage takers, had formed a kind of Think Tank and he performed a public opinion poll in Iran a couple of years ago. He reached the conclusion that a great majority of Iranians wanted good relations with the USA. He and his close associates were immediately arrested and charged with espionage. After interrogation, it took no time for a few of Abdi's colleagues to "remember" that they had been US spies in Iran and they confessed and apologized.

The people of Iran, along with the people of the USA, have never forgotten the criminal actions of those who committed and supported this heinous act and they look forward to the day that these elements are put to criminal trial.

Notes:

(1)http://en.wikipedia.org/wiki/Alexandr_Griboyedov. "...Several months after his wedding to the 16-year-old daughter of his friend Prince Chavchavadze, Griboedov was suddenly sent to Persia as Minister Plenipotentiary. Soon after his arrival at Tehran, a crowd of Islamic religious fanatics stormed the Russian embassy. Griboyedov (along with almost everyone else inside) was slaughtered...."

(2) Almost all of these groups were feeling obliged to perform espionage work for the USSR, as the mother state. Some of these groups had practiced the takeover of the embassy in another occasion. The Tudeh part of Iran was a communist party and it was clear that it had to act in that way. The Fadiian Khalgh was openly Marxist Leninist. The MKO's links to the leftist groups was very much exposed in the issue of "Sa'adati". He was a person who had been arrested red handed while delivering some classified documents to the Russian agents. The MKOs of that time, which were very different from the present ones, tried vigorously to prove that "there was not a case of espionage". But eventually Assadolah Lajevardi, the Bucher of Evin, killed Sa'adati. The MKOs of that juncture were always insisting that the American hostages should be put to trial.

(3) R. K. Ramazani, Iran's Hostage Crisis: International Legitimacy Matters, Comparative Studies of South Asia, Africa and the Middle East, Duke University Press, Vol. 25, No.2, 2005, pp. 273-278.

(4) A website close to the Expediency Council in Iran.

(5) http://www.baztab.ir/news/52218.php, dated 11/4/2006, this is an article by Mehdi Salimi, in the Baztab website that belongs to influential circles in Islamic regime of Iran, the article, in Farsi, is under the title of " Who was the winner: Iran or the USA?" And it is a review of the incident.

(6) On the 24th of March, Carter wrote a confidential letter to Imam Khomeini and mentioned: "we are ready to accept the new realities that have emerged out of the Iranian revolution. This is a constant aim for us. I believe that both of us are following the same aim, which is the universal peace and justice for all nations." (Refer to: http://www.baztab.ir/news/52218.php, dated 11/4/2006, Mehdi Salimi, in the Baztab website.)

(7) http://www.cjr/issues/2004/6/letter-berkeley-siamdoust.asp?printerfriendly=yes

(8) http://news.gooya.com/politics/archives/2006/11/054389print.php, dated 11/06/2006

(9) Massoumeh Ebtekar, Takeover in Tehran: the inside story of the 1979 US Embassy Capture, Canada, Talonbooks, 2000.

SAFETY OF THE NUCLEAR FACILITIES OF IRAN: A FORGOTTEN DIMENSION

The political and security dimensions of the Iranian nuclear case have been so hot that one of the most important aspects of this program is constantly ignored by the people of Iran, other countries and even the IAEA. This dimension is the safety dimension of the Iranian declared and undeclared nuclear facilities. Here are some of the general questions that come to mind:

How safe are the nuclear facilities in the sites that are known and unknown to the public?

What is the radiation level of the nuclear materials at these facilities?

What kinds of radiations are emitted from these facilities?

What is done with the nuclear wastes at these sites, are they kept in the site, or they transferred to somewhere else? How is the transfer done?

What are the procedures for the sea, air and road transportation of the hazardous materials related to the construction and fuel cycle of the nuclear facilities?

What accidents have already occurred at these facilities and what were their consequences inside and outside of the facilities?

What are the safety standards of the existing instruments in these facilities?

What plans are in place for emergency situations like melt down of the reactors due to malfunction of its main parts, natural incidents, or similar events?

Which organizations are ready for tackling the accidents such as "specialized fires" at these facilities?

How well are these facilities able to withstand an earthquake especially given that some of them may be in areas on the earthquake belt?

How do these disclosed and undisclosed nuclear facilities impact the region where they are located in terms of the environment and ecology?

What are standards and the actual situation of the storage facilities for the nuclear materials?

What are the chances of these facilities against terrorism, theft, and organized crime activities?

What are the software and hardware safety levels of the nuclear facilities?

What are the applicable safety laws and regulations at the nuclear facilities and who is in charge of implementation and verifying implementation of those laws?

What are the safety and environmental consequences of an attack against the presently declared nuclear sites in Iran?

As an example, it is a well-known fact that the Amirabad Area in the northwest of Tehran is seriously under the radiations of the Nuclear Reactor of Tehran University in the same area. (When the concerned reactor was established, Amirabad was in the suburbs of Tehran but at the moment it is in the middle of the city. Most probably, many other areas around Amirabad get the same radiations in various levels). The Iranian officials never talk about the dangers of these radiations.

In the past, sometimes in the scientific contexts, they have claimed that the level of radiation from the Amirabad Nuclear

Reactor is one that poses no danger to the public. However, they may change their views about the level of the radiation that is OK for the people. The people of Iran, especially the people living in Tehran are well aware of the regime's irresponsibility and lack of consideration when it comes to the level of radiation that is harmful for the inhabitants of the concerned areas.

As far as I know the radiation from the nuclear facilities of Amirabad nuclear reactor (which is a very old reactor and has never been fully maintained. Perhaps it is the time to close it and use a better technology as compared to this forty year technology) has been the subject of a couple of studies in Iran and their results have never been made public out of fear of creating chaos. In fact, if the safety problems of Iran's nuclear facilities and how the Iranian government has approached (or failed to correctly address) these dangerous problems were exposed the people's reaction to this issue may cause the nuclear case of Iran to take a different turn from the inside without the need for foreign involvement.

According to the report of the Global Security Organization: "Since 1968, the Tehran Nuclear Research Center [located in suburban Amirabad] has included a research reactor with a nominal capacity of 5 megawatts provided by the United States under. The reactor was due to be upgraded and replaced with Argentine's assistance in the late 1980s... there are unconfirmed reports that this facility can produce plutonium from spent nuclear fuel.... Iran, acknowledged the receipt in 1991 of natural uranium, which had not been reported previously to the Agency [IAEA].... which was now being stored at the previously undeclared Jaber Ibn Hayan Multipurpose Laboratories (JHL) located at the Tehran Nuclear Research Center." (1)

However, the research nuclear reactor of Tehran University, which is based on an American design, is less dangerous than the Chernobyl type nuclear reactors exported by the Russians. The Chernobyl accident showed the disaster that a flawed design of the Russian reactors could create. According to the report of the CRS: "The Chernobyl accident was by far the worst nuclear power plant accident to have occurred anywhere in the world.

At least 31 persons died quickly from acute radiation exposure or other injuries, and between 5,000 and 45,000 fatal cancers may result over the next 40 years from radiation released during the accident. Those cancers would represent an increase in the cancer rate of about half a percent among the 75 million people in the western part of the former Soviet Union and a smaller increase in non-Soviet Europe, with a higher increase possible in the contaminated region around the planet.

The 10-year anniversary of the Chernobyl accident prompted renewed interest in the disaster's long-term consequences. According to a November 1995 report by the Organization for Economic Cooperation and Development (OECD), the primary observable health consequence of the accident has been a dramatic increase in childhood thyroid cancer. About 1,000 cases of childhood thyroid cancer have been reported in certain regions surrounding the destroyed reactor -- a rate that is as much as a hundred times the pre-accident level, according to OECD. The death rate for accident cleanup workers has also risen measurably, the organization reported. Other recent studies have found increased genetic mutations among children born in contaminated regions.

Environmental contamination from the accident was widespread. The OECD report estimated that about 50,000 square miles of land in Belarus, Ukraine, and Russia were substantially contaminated with radioactive cesium. Significant levels of radioactive strontium, plutonium, and other isotopes were also deposited. Although radiation levels have declined during the past decade, land-use restrictions in the most contaminated areas may remain indefinitely, according to OECD." (2)

It is noteworthy that the effects of the Chernobyl accidents were detected in the cities of Iran in the southern shores of the Caspian Sea, especially in Ramsar. Due to the good relations of the existing Islamic regime of Iran with the Russians, the real extent of these effects was never revealed. After all the Russians are polluting the Caspian Sea with so much radioactive waste that as compared with them this is nothing. The former Soviet states, especially Kazakhstan and Azerbaijan, have been the storage places for the Russian nuclear wastes which is stored in substandard conditions; in the past, these materials have polluted and contaminated the waters of the Caspian Sea as a result of nuclear waste leaked from the storages and this is still a source of environmental and safety danger for the Caspian Sea.

According to NIT Nuclear Trafficking Database: "The main radioactive waste storage facility in Azerbaijan is the Izotop Industrial Complex, located 30km from Baku. Izotop was constructed in the 1950s and holds 510 tanks of radioactive waste in 10 storage tanks designed to hold only low-level radioactive waste. However, as of March 2000, nine of the 10 tanks were full and, in many cases, the level of radiation is above 1,000 roentgens. Data collected before 1988 suggest that approximately 350 organizations have a total of 950 radiation sources in their possession. These organizations include military facilities, research institutes, production plants and health services-related enterprises.

Spent radioactive sources from these organizations never reached the Izotop storage facility. Instead they are spread throughout the Baku region. Out of 157 radioactive contamination sites discovered in 1988 as a result of a special inspection in the Baku region, only 31 had been cleaned as of early 1996. Many of these radioactive sources were left behind by the chemical weapons divisions stationed in Baku, Lenkoran, Gyandzha and Nakhichevan during the Soviet period." (3)

The handling of the nuclear materials in the laboratorial level I (as is the case with many hazardous materials including chemical and microbiological elements) is one thing, and handling them in the industrial or mass level is quite a different issue. The main difference in these two levels is the issue of safety. The handling of the nuclear materials, buildings, personnel, wastes, transportation and so on is subject to many complicated procedures. I doubt that many of the sites that have been operating in the concealed location or even the known location would have the necessary safety standards.

While it is true that as of 1993 Iran is a member of the United Nations Convention on the Control of Trans boundary Movement of the Hazardous Wastes and Their Disposal (Bazel Convention) (the Bazel Convention was put in force in 1992) it is not clear at all that the detailed regulations of this convention are observed for transportation of the hazardous materials to and from the nuclear facilities of Iran, especially the undeclared ones.

I have never seen the reports of the IAEA and others in the last several years that the nuclear program of Iran has been in the limelight to address the issue of safety in the nuclear facilities of Iran. Can the IAEA say how many persons inside and outside of the facilities they have inspected have died due to mishandling of the nuclear materials? What trainings have been provided to the people for example living within a certain radius from the nuclear power plant of Bushehr, Isfahan USF facilities, the uranium extracting sites, and Natanaz facilities? Where is the waste of the nuclear facilities of Iran and under what conditions are they stored? Are the people in the concerned regions aware that they are living near dangerous materials? How come you see a warning posted near electricity poles: "danger" or "keep out" due to dangers of electrical cables or wires, but there is no similar warnings for the highly dangerous nuclear facilities?

It is interesting for the people of the concerned areas to know that if the nuclear program of Iran goes towards the military side (many experts believe that the nuclear program of Iran is definitely military and doubt that the government of the Islamic regime of Iran would be actually concerned about getting electricity for its people in the next fifty years) then the problems of safety about production and storage and use of the explosive nuclear materials get worse. I can say with certainty that a high percentage of activities in the nuclear facilities of the nuclear powers are devoted to the issue of safety of production, use and storage of the nuclear materials.

The nuclear technology is brought from the underground organizations like the Khan Network in Pakistan and Malaysia, along with the know-how taken from the Russians and Koreans. It is not clear how safe these technologies are and there is doubt that the Russians or Koreans are ready to give Iran the best technology that they may have.

The American and international sanctions against the nuclear program of Iran have created difficulties for the program and sometimes the "Iranian scientists" have found "special ways" to solve these problems in their own limited and unchecked framework. God knows to how much danger these "special solutions" will expose the people and personnel of these facilities. Who will be liable for their mistakes? What kind of protection will the people of the concerned areas have against accidents, mistakes, human errors and design flaws of these facilities?

The Bushehr reactor, according to Morteza Aminmansour is suffering from "...Substandard plant instrumentation and controls. Wiring of emergency electrical systems and reactor safety functions are inter connected in ways that allow failure of a control system to prevent operation of the safety system. Quality control, design and construction are significantly deficient by US standards.... Secrecy is the biggest enemy of nuclear safety and international isolation could result in significant risks for Iran's nuclear industry..." (4)

The Safety of the nuclear facilities in Iran is an important matter for the people of Iran, and the neighboring countries in the case of a military attack by missiles or aerial bombardment. If the nuclear reactor of Bushehr Power Plant starts its operation and is destroyed due to military attacks, the effects of the radiations from an operational reactor will not be limited to Iran and most of the states in the Persian Gulf area may become affected. The possible effects may reach American troops in Iraq.

The government of the Islamic regime of Iran has been concealing the locations and activities of the nuclear program of Iran for many years. However, the important issue of the safety of the nuclear sites and consequences of the concealed activities without proper supervision (to detect and remove the safety problems) has been forgotten by all sides.

Notes:

(1) http://www.globalsecurity.org/wmd/world/iran/terhran-tnrc.html

(2) http://enie.org/NLE/CRSreports/energy/eng-5.efm

(3) http://www.nti.org/e_research/profiles/Azerbaijan/index_4666.html

(4) http://www.iranian.ws/egi-bin/Iran_news/exec/view.egi/2/2/2182

PRIVATIZATION IN IRAN

The Supreme Leader of the Islamic regime of Iran has issued a command to the Government of Iran regarding transfer of 80 percent of several governmental companies to the private sector of Iran. The question comes to mind: what is the motive behind the moves of the Supreme Leader? My answers are:

1- Giving the impression that the regime of Iran is moving in the direction of capitalism, while the regime of Iran is suspected of being a communist-type economy. The private sector is very weak in Iran. In fact, there is no private sector in Iran. Aside from small businesses in the market, the entire economy is under the government control. The current private sector of Iran is an artificial continuation of the public sector. In other words, the people who have the political power give hints to their affiliates to establish apparently private companies in order to serve the governmental agencies. For example, the people who control the Ministry of Jihad (a parallel organization to the Ministry of Agriculture and an organization that takes decisions and implements them without regular scrutiny under the pretext of being revolutionary and in fact, a cover for the corrupt and ignorant managers of the regime in this field) give to their relatives the contracts for purchasing millions of dollars of medicines for animals. These relatives then establish a front company and act as if they are the private sector. The new company buys large amount of drugs (usually from the worst places with artificially fixed prices and under the worst possible contractual conditions, but contain lucrative advantages for the "private persons" involved, like fellowships to Western universities, travel to special places with fully paid packages and so on).

2- Putting the blame for economic failure on the private sector. The regime has failed in the field of economic affairs more than other fields and this is an opportunity to blame the private sector for the upcoming waves of unemployment, low level productions, high inflation, rising prices, and all other economic issues the regime faces. The reality is that since the Islamic Revolution, many of the governmental companies are operating at a loss. Lack of proper management, high corruption, and many other issues are there. Right from the beginning of the so-called Islamic Revolution, the regime has confiscated the private companies. Those that had good chances of making profits (due to the exclusive status they enjoy), have been given to the Bonyads or foundations. Those that are on the loss side have been collected in an organization called the "Organization of the National Industries". Now these companies are going to be offered to the people in the stock market.

The reality is that the problem of Islamic Republic of ran is not the privatization of the state companies, the country needs to eradicate the Supreme Leader. This figure and the establishment under his command are the sources of misery for the country and they should be eliminated. Democracy and freedom ask eradication of the institution of the Supreme leadership.

IRAN AND ALL ISLAMIC NATIONS NEED SERIOUS SECULARISM

D r. Abdulkarim Soroush, a prominent Iranian-Islamic scholar confessed in a speech in Paris (http://news. gooya.com/society/archieves/034301.php) that Islam has no political and civil rights for the people. What you find in the Islamic jurisprudence is only obligations, not rights. There-fore, it is useless to look for democracy in Islam.

These remarks are new attestation to the long time proven prin-ciple that religion must be separated from politics. This is espe-cially true in the case of Islam. Secularism is the medicine acutely needed in all the Islamic societies, especially in Iran.

The experience of Islamic revolution in Iran proved once again that the mixture of politics and Islam in world that is divided into nation-states and governments designed to follow national inter-ests, does not work. For a long time in Iran (hundreds of years), religious people had claimed that all societal problems came from non-observance of Islamic rules and if religious Islamic leaders become political masters in the society, everything would be in order and justice would prevail all over the state.

More than three decades of Islamic government in Iran has showed clearly that the idea is not working. There is no doubt that the people of Iran are less religious and more underde-veloped now as compared to thirty years ago. Many people in

Islamic societies are trying to separate their religion from politics. What is happening in Iran at the present juncture is a clear struggle by the people of Iran to separate religion from politics.

There is no other way. Anyone, including the Muslims and any government, especially the U.S., that wish a better life for the people of Islamic countries and similar states, which also seek international peace and development in the world should help the cause of separating religion from politics.

Jalal Al-Ahmad, the Iranian writer that the regime of the Islamic Republic of Iran tries to claim as its own, has said: there are two groups that cannot be intellectual: the clergymen and the military men. (http://news.gooya.com/president84/archives/030995. php)

The term national-religious is an oxymoron and these so called national religious groups which have become active in Iran in recent years accomplish nothing because they lack a real understanding of the nationalistic as well as religious goals; these national religious groups claim to be intellectuals and at the same time religious but they are intellectuals who are incapable of thinking outside the box, like Ali Shariati and Mehdi Bazaghan. Ali Sharati, who was called a "spy" by Dr. Beheshti, one of the founders of the Islamic regime of Iran who was killed in a bombing accident, along with people like Bazarghan, is responsible for deceiving at least the past two generations in Iran. Fortunately, the present young generation of Iran is too smart to fall for the tactics of people such as Shariati and his fellow travelers. This "shop" is closed.

However, the victims of these demagogues have the responsibility to reveal the mistakes so history would not repeat itself. The combination of nationalistic ideas and religion does not work. Those who are pretending otherwise are liars. Religions, especially Islam, are not able to support democracy. Religions by nature are tyrannical.

The expansionist religions, like Islam, follow a kind of universalism that gives the monopoly of power to the religious despots and their interpretation of the religion. People, like Ali Shariati, are responsible for creating something out of Islam that did not exist at its inception and it does not matter whether or not they themselves believed this absurd theory or used it as a strategy to achieve other goals; they are nonetheless demagogues that have deceived the people.

The members of this group had a great role in the hijacking of the Iranian Revolution (which was after freedom and justice) by the religious zealots and their ignorant thugs. It is interesting that many members of this group are now considered as a kind of reformist of the mess that they have created. The present regime of Iran knows these demagogues better than anybody else.

These are the direct words of Hassan Abbasi, the Director of Center of External Security Analysis of the Revolutionary Guards Corps, talking in the Tehran University (05/23/04):

"The leaders of the Islamic world should have the courage to declare: Islam and Western democracy are not compatible. Islam has nothing in common with the Universal Declaration of the Human Rights. Islam has nothing in common with the Western liberalism and this kind of freedom. Islam opposes these ideas... According to Nietzsche, the founding of a civil society leads to the death of God...the Koran has said: go to war...if it is possible to do something that the disbelievers feel fearful, and then this kind of terrorism is holy terrorism.... Look at my hands. These are the hands that have created Hizbullah, Hamas and Islamic Jihad... You have 6000 nuclear warheads... those are our target. The guerrillas will destroy them.... We are working on recruiting the Mexicans and Argentineans for our cause... We will mobilize everyone who has a complaint against the America...we have identified all of their weak points... and we will give those information to the combatant groups of the world." (http://khbabarnameh.gooya.com/nabavi/archives/real/abbasi-hassan.rm)

The Muslim people are sick and tired of religious extremism. Religion is a personal thing and it should be private. Whoever tries to impose religion on the people should be properly stopped. Imposing ideas is against the freedom of expression and a violation of the people's rights. Unfortunately, the Government of Iran that does not represent the people of Iran has taken policies that are against the Iranian ideas and interests. The Government of Iran, which has taken the power through a creeping coup called "the Second invasion of Iran by the Arabs", has been killing itself during the last 30 years to make the people more Islamic but all those efforts are in vain. The people of Iran at the moment are less Islamic than the time of the previous regime. The regime has taken so many steps visibly and invisibly to impose, attract, lure, and make people interested in or push them toward Islam and it has failed. Some of the measures were:

* Promoting the Arabic language in Iran under the pretext of the Koran

* Publishing religious books in millions of copies every year and distributing them free of charge inside and outside of Iran

* Changing the program of the schools and universities by including religious materials, inserting distorted historical stories (based on the fake sources) in text books, giving higher priority for getting good grades in courses related to Islamic studies

* Imposing the laws of the ancient Arab nomads under the name of Islam on the judicial system of Iran

* Establishment of hundreds of Islamic theological schools all over the country that produce thousands of a certain types of narrow-minded graduates, with or without turbans, every year.

* Expansion of the Islamic rituals like the special congregational prayers (like Friday prayer) under the supervision of the hard-line and non-understanding Mullahs.

* Expansion of Islamic propaganda inside and outside the country by using the mass media, especially the radio, TV and cinema.

* Creation of a kind of division between the people that are called "the insiders" and "the outsiders". The insiders are the herd-mentality followers of Islam as interpreted by the regime and they are considered as human beings that have some limited

rights. The outsiders are worse than animals. The regime does not care who does what to the outsiders.

* Adding the word "Islamic" to all governmental and non-government institutions in order to create limitations for the managers

* Clear prejudice in favor of the small minority of Iranians that follow the Islamic gibberish of the regime. Even most of this minority does not believe in what is indoctrinated by the regime as Islam.

* Trying to disconnect Iranians from their glorious past.

Iran is ready to accept secularism as the best option for moving towards democracy. Any person that opposes this option wants to delay the movement of Iran towards democracy at least 400 years (the time of renaissance in Europe). Religion should be separated from state administration. A special organ should be established to find and discard the religious influence from state affairs.

Iran needs a period of De-Islamization. Iran, contrary to what many Westerners think, is not a deeply Islamic country. The people of Iran are not serious Muslims and they do not intend to be so. What Iran and all Islamic nations need is serious secularism.

TAZIR: THE ISLAMIC
TORTURE IN IRAN

Torture has close relationship with ideological zealotry. In the justice system of the Islamic Republic of Iran, a special word has been chosen to replace "Shekangheh" (the Persian word for torture) with the Arabic word of "Tazir". This is not a simple change of words. The initiative to put Tazir in the place of shekanjeh meaning torture has serious and important implications for the IRI judicial system and the people who appear before the court.

The word Tazir is devised to clear the conscience of the interrogators, especially in the Islamic Revolutionary Courts, and their masters that clearly believe in all kinds of torture as an instrument of the administration of justice. The Mullahs and their lackeys can pretend, under the pretext of "Tazir", that they are not involved in torture. All Iranian judicial officials claim that there is no torture in Iran (outright denial is one of the simple answers of the official of the Islamic regime of Iran to many questions: Lajevardi, the Butcher of Evin, used to say there was no political prisoner in Iran.) but what they really mean is that there is no act called "torture" in the prisons and interrogation centers of the regime and yet if you ask what about "Tazir", the response is Tazir cannot be torture because it is applied on the basis of the ruling of the religious judicial officials.

The reality is that there is no civil justice system in Islamic regime of Iran. The Islamic Revolutionary Courts look into all important issues, including all crimes against the security of the regime, major economic cases, and the cases related to the narcotic drugs and socials vices like drinking alcoholic beverages or having a party with the members of the opposite sex in any form. It is useless to say something is "law" in the Islamic Republic of Iran because the Islamic Revolutionary Courts work according to the rulings of the Ayatollahs (called Fatwas and collected in books called Resalah) and the laws legitimated in the so-called Majles on the basis of the same rulings. Rule of law becomes meaningless when the violations of human rights and denial of the fundamental rights are actually part and parcel of the laws adopted by the Majles.

The judges, according to Islamic law only have to be Mullahs to be qualified and they judge according to what they claim to be "the law" of Islam. When an interrogator wants to torture a person, especially the political ones, he goes to a mullah-judge (called Hakem-e Shariah) and asks him to give permission for let's say inflicting 50 lashes to get a confession from a suspect. If that works, mission is accomplished. If not, he can go back and get permission from the mullah- judge for additional and harsher lashings.

There is obviously a great difference in terms of pain between a gentle lash stroke and the severe stroke that would cause blood to gush out of the body of the miserable tortured person; however, there are no criteria or system to administer or observe how the permission of "Tazir" is implemented. The interrogators implement them as they wish. Sometimes the lashing, especially against women and young prisoners lead to severe injuries, damaging the internal organs and permanent loss of the physical functions. The interrogators never say that are involved in torture. Even a professional torturer like Assadollah Lajevardi, the Butcher of Evin, always spoke against torture and condemned the judicial system of the former Shah of Iran and the judicial system of other countries for having torture in their systems. His disciples that now rule the judicial system of Iran always use

"Tazir" for getting confessions. They claim that they observe the constitutional law of Iran which forbids torture and they only execute the religious orders of the mullah judges for "Tazir'.

The mullah judges never dare to ask the interrogators who the persons that will be subjected to "Tazir" are. Tazir in the interrogation chambers of the judicial system of Iran consists of the same methods that are traditionally used in all places under the title of "torture and degrading and cruel treatments". Long solitary confinement is not at all considered torture, when in fact according to experts even short periods of solitary imprisonment are torture and it is one of the worst kinds of torture.

Other forms of Tazir in Iran are: fastening the person to an iron bed and lashing in the sole of feet, lashing the back of a person, beating the individual with a piece of cable, hanging the person upside down. One of the favorite "Tazirs" of the disciplinary forces is called "Chicken Kebab".

They fasten the person to a pole and turn and beat the person on the soles of feet and the person's back at the same time. There are other forms of torture too like stopping the medications, leaving the light on in the cells for 24 hours, calling for interrogation at odd times like middle of night, calling the person for interrogation while the eyes are closed by special blind folds and then leaving the person for long hours (for example 5 in the morning to 8 in the evening) without doing anything for several days, putting the person in a cell with insane or sick people, or hard criminals, threatening to arrest the person's family, taking the members of family as hostage, sending the person to other prisons far from the residence, misusing the sentence of "exile", misuse of the prisoner's pay by prison officials, encouraging all prisoners to read Koran and learn it by heart irrespective of whether or not the prisoner is a Muslim which infringes on the rights of religious minorities. These methods are applied against men and women and it seems when it comes to torture (Tazir) the Islamic Republic of Iran does not discriminate.

THE ROOTS OF UNREST AMONG THE IRANIAN MINORITIES

The unrest among Iranian minorities that form a considerable part of the Iranian population is the result of:

1- The failure of the Islamic regime to implement its Constitutionals Law. This issue is not limited to the rights of the minorities. Although the Constitutional Law of the Islamic Republic of Iran itself is for the most part against any rule of law, democracy and human rights (mainly due to the articles related to the Supreme Leader as a person with all powers and no responsibility), the Islamic regime of Iran does not bother to even comply with its own laws. In fact, some of the Iranian reformists in the past did not ask for anything further than the implementation of the Iranian Constitutional Law.

2- The failure of the Islamic regime to answer to the demands of the Iranian society, including the minorities, for the democracy, rule of law, separation of the politics and religion. The people of Iran are not serious religious persons and the regime of the Islamic Republic has been acting against the wishes and demands of the people. The Islamic Republic has already lost the limited legitimacy that it had in the beginning of the revolution.

3- Serious violation of human nights of all Iranians as envisaged in the Universal Declaration of Human rights (and the UN Conventions on the Civil, political, social and economic rights).

The Islamic regime of Iran, as the successor to the previous regime, is legally responsible to observe the above documents that were signed and adopted by the government of Iran. However, since the revolution, the religious regime of Iran has tried to undermine these important documents.

4- Suppression of the minorities and violation of their ethnic and cultural rights and ignoring their demands. The religious and ethnic minorities have been subject to double suppression in the Islamic regime. Failure to answer these rights and demands, and denial of such rights under the pretext of conspiracy theories, alien involvement, and acts that will lead to the country's disintegration (whether claimed by the regime or the opposition) will not solve any problem and must be properly addressed.

5- Failure of the Islamic regime to get reformed. The Islamic regime has dominated the Iranian people for the last 30 years. The people of Iran are clearly sick and tired of the regime that does not even acknowledge a commitment to the national interests of Iran. The people of Iran hoped that after the election of the previous president (Khatami), a new chapter would be opened through introduction of some reforms in the line of civil society and democracy. The failure of the previous president and emergence of the new government that has openly declared its policy of going back to the early years of the Revolution has made the people of Iran deeply disappointed about the prospects of reforms in the country. The actions taken by the government, especially the repressive measures have not succeeded to stop the unrest. It seems that these troubles are there to stay in the Islamic regime as long as the regime proves to be opposed to any reform. After the rigged elections that brought the new president to power, the people of Iran, including the minorities, have lost their hope for reform inside the Islamic regime and in order to get their fair share of the governments the minorities are seeking a way out which may result in disintegration of Iran.

6- Insistence of the Islamic regime on the issues which are not important for the Iranian society (such as expansion of Islam, the situation of the Palestinians, expansion of the ancient nomadic culture through religious texts in Iran, payment of money and providing assistance to the terrorist and non-terrorist groups under the pretext of expanding Islam, intervention in the affairs of other countries due to the presumed duty of the regime and so on).

7- The ethnic minorities of Iran, like all people of Iran, are under suppression and their rights are violated. The fact that ethnic minorities may have relations with their ethnic groups in other countries (such as the Republic of Azerbaijan in the case of Azeris, the Iraqi Kurdistan in the case of Kurds, the Pakistan's Baluchestan in the case of Baluchis, Turkmenistan Republic in the case of the Iranian Turkamans, and the Persian Gulf states and Iraq in the case of the Iranian Arab tribes) has made the situation more troublesome for the regime. As far as Azerbaijan is concerned, two movements under the titles of Pan-Azeri and Pan-Turkish are active in the region. Certain groups support the Pan-Azeri movement in the Republic of Azerbaijan and the Iranian Azerbaijan. Turkey orchestrates the second one. These groups are also tools of the two concerned countries (Azerbaijan Republic and Turkey) for checking the intervention of the Islamic regime in their affairs and possible plans for the export of the religious zealots under the pretext of preaching for religious purposes.

8- There is some support for disintegration of Iran through outside powers. The Russians have been historically happy and they have always welcomed disintegration of Iran because it gives them more power for maneuvers on political issues of the region. Also, there are inclinations in the West to see Iran's disintegration to put an end to the regime that threatens the world and continues to insist on its nuclear military program.

9- Continuation of the suppressive Islamic regime of Iran and failure of the Islamic regime's internal plans, along with the historical grievances are pushing the Iranian minorities towards the forces of disintegration. The minorities, like other people of Iran, are seeking for a way to get rid of the domination of an inhumane regime and unfortunately disintegration seems a suitable way for them. If the people of Iran do not succeed to topple the Islamic regime (with or without outside help), they are going to suffer the damages of disintegration. After all, is it better to stay a part of Iran and be destroyed by the Islamic regime or the American-Israeli attack or start a new life like many newly-established countries of the world?

WHAT IS PROBLEM OF SUFIS IN IRAN?

The regime of Iran has always looked with suspicion and sometimes disgust on the Sufis because the Dervishes do not believe in any role for the Mullahs. They believe that people do not need any middleman for contacting God. The Dervishes are very devoted to their way of life. They see the religious zealots as corrupt people.

However, these are not the reason of the attacks against them. The real reason is that the people of Iran, especially younger generations, out of desperation or any other reason, are welcoming the Sufi gatherings more and more. When the Sufis had their gathering in the past they tried to stay away from politics. Welcoming of the Sufi ways of life and the Sufi type of approach to religion (especially towards Islam) has found a new wave during the recent years. Every year, more and more people try to have gatherings under the name of Sufis.

Some of these "gatherings" are only an excuse for resisting the strict Islamic and ideological interpretations of the Mullahs in Iran and therefore they are not simple religious or mystic (or combination of both of them) sessions. They are a kind of centers for resistance of the people and rejection of the Mullahs and they are little by little getting more members and at the same time, they are becoming more political.

Problems of the Islamic Republic of Iran

The new stage of Islamic fundamentalism, after the election of the new president by the mafia regime of the Iranian mullahs, has opened the way for the organized street thugs (like Basijis) and the disciplinary forces to make trouble for the Sufis, disrupt their gatherings and destroy their places of worship. This new wave of attacks against the Iranian Sufis is based on the regime sensing danger about the possibility of new moves under the name of Sufis against the Mullahs and their lackeys.

Sufis have always been respected in Iran because of their humble and down to earth behavior. Definitely their approach to life is different from the dictatorial imposition of the special interpretation of Islam by the Mullahs of Iran. Some of the people in Iran have found a way of getting away from the rulings of the Mullahs through adherence to Sufi practices. The Sufis are among the most peace-loving and tolerant people in Iran and probably in the world. They are suffering under the Iranian regime and they consider such suffering as part of the duty that they owe to their faith. Perhaps it is time that Iranian Sufis change their approach and open a new way for the younger generations seeking refuge in them.

Iran-US: Meaning
of Mutual Respect

Negotiations between Iran and United States, whether it gets to a compromise or not, are in the making. The two sides have expressed readiness for negotiation on the basis of mutual respect. However, it seems that they do not agree on the meaning of this word.

The package proposed by the Government of the Islamic Republic of Iran in response to the P5+1 has reiterated that: "...commitment to the Mutual Respect, justice and rule of law can open the way for a new stage of negotiations for materialization of the long term cooperation in the direction of consolidating the sustainable peace and security in the regional and global levels." (1)

At the same time, President Obama had said in his message to the Iranian people and rulers on the occasion of Nowruz: "... My administration is committed to diplomacy that addresses the full range of issues before us, and to pursuing constructive ties among the United States, Iran and the international community. This process will not be advanced by threats. We seek instead engagement that is honest and grounded in mutual respect." (2) President Obama has said earlier, "in the coming months he will be looking for ways to open direct talks with Iran geared towards developing a relationship of mutual respect". (3) Almost the same day Iran's President, Ahmadinejad, said the country was ready for dialogue under a just climate and "mutual respect". (4)

So, are they talking about the same thing?

"Mutual Respect" has been a signature phrase of the Islamic Republic for years. Former UN Ambassador Javad Zarif used the line regularly, as did Iran's former Foreign Minister Kamal Kharazzi, and former presidents Rafsanjani and Khatami. Ahmadinejad even used the phrase in an interview with state media while he was still Mayor of Tehran and running for President. Former Iran's Foreign Ministry spokesman Dr. Hamidreza Assefi elaborated on Iran's concept of "mutual respect" in a May 2003 session with local reporters: "Mutual respect has a clear meaning. Iran expects the US to follow the principle of 'mutual respect' toward the Islamic Republic by refraining from interfering in Iran's internal affairs, accepting the principle of equality, and living up to the requirements of mutual respect..." (5) Ahmadinejad said recently...I tell those who say they want to create change: this is change: apologize to the nation of Iran and try to make up for their dark history and crimes they have committed against the Iranian nation. We welcome change but on the condition that the change is fundamental... if a real change occurs in a fundamental way, we shall welcome." (6)

These are exactly the points that he said in his congratulatory letter to Obama on the occasion of his victory in the presidential elections. He said: "... the opportunities that God create are limited and you should take this opportunity to leave a good name for yourself. Nations of the world are longing that the policies based on warmongering, occupation, force, deception, humiliation, and imposed discriminatory and unjust relations are set aside and instead of them, they want to see the respect for peoples and nations rights, friendship, and non-intervention in others affairs..." (7)

Ali Larijani, Majles Speaker, addressing the security conference in Munich on 6th of Feb. 2009 said: "here is the list of our grievances against the USA:

1- The US arranged 1952 Coup against the national government of Mossadegh.

2- The US sent a delegation headed by General Hazier to Iran in 1979 to arrange a coup.

3- After the Islamic revolution, the US orchestrated separatist and terrorist movements through its embassy in Tehran.

4- The US pushed Saddam to attack Iran.

5- The US confiscated Iran's properties in the early days of the revolution.

6- The US violated its nuclear agreement with Iran in the early days of the revolution and did not act according to its commitments for delivering the fuel for the Tehran nuclear reactor.

7- Under the pretext of combating terrorism and WMD occupied Iraq and Afghanistan.

8- The 33 days of war in Lebanon was planned and executed by the US assistance.

9- The unjust 22 days of war in the Gaza was accompanied with all out US help.

10- In the nuclear case of Iran, the US has been the main trouble maker and the party that created stumbling blocks in the diplomatic ways of solving the crisis.

He also, proposed four ways to tackle the global issues:

1- The US must stop unilateralism.

2- The East has different conditions due to various reasons. The Islamic revival in the Middle Eastern states is not a phenomenon that you can tackle with through negation of facts. The world today needs a reasonable, just and realistic theory for security.

3- Domineering and terrorism are two sides of the same coin. The era of dominance of the West over East is over.

4- Instead of following the unrealistic patterns, the US must respect the regional specifications. (8)

H. Shariatmadari, the editor of Kayhan, talking about Ahmadine-jad's speech which was widely reported as Iran's readiness for direct talks to the US, said:

"The reference of our respected president regarding readiness of Iran for negotiations with the USA in his speech on the occasion of 22nd of Bahman [anniversary of the Islamic revolution on 12 Feb] had extensive coverage in the political and media circles of the West...president said: " in order to walk towards negotiations the change must be real and fundamental, not tactical. The people of Iran welcome real changes. The people of Iran are ready to talk but in an atmosphere of justice and mutual respect. It seems that Mr. Ahmadinejad was trying to respond to the trick of the new US president and by putting emphasis on two expressions of "justice and mutual respect", which have no place in the jargon of the USA, he tried to reveal the true face of the USA for the public opinions of the world. This incentive is respectful per se. How-ever, with all due regards to the president of our state, I have to say the remarks of our president was contrary to his revolution-ary incentive and his expectations are only playing in the enemy's field. It is necessary that that they are corrected immediately and in a wise way. This wrong thinking should not be created [out of his words] that the Islamic Republic of Iran had made a revision in its revolutionary, logical and dignified stances..." (9)

He meant that there was no change in Iran's position and what Ahmadinejad has said under the title of "mutual respect" con-tains all of Iran's grievances. In response to the question of what is mutual respect in the Iranian diplomacy, a prominent Iranian-American scholar, Professor R. K. Ramazani (Professor Emeritus of Government and Foreign Affairs at the University of Virginia) has said:

"First, respect means that American negotiators should recog-nize Iran's fierce sense of independence. The Iranian people remember repeated foreign invasion, occupation, interference, dictation and domination during many tumultuous centuries. Second, respect means the United States should acknowledge that Iran has strategic importance and is a major player in the

Middle East, particularly in the Persian Gulf region, where it straddles the Strait of Hormuz, the global oil chokepoint; where it connects the Middle East to Central Asia and South Asia. Third, respect means that the United States should treat Iran on the basis of equality. ..Iranians resent that the United States has imposed untold economic and diplomatic sanctions on Iran; has sided with Saddam Hussein's regime against Iran in the Iraq-Iran War; has shot down an Iranian passenger plane over the Persian Gulf, killing 290 people; has depicted Iran as the world's greatest sponsor of terrorism; has called for regime change; has threatened military strikes on Iran's nuclear facilities in Natanz, and has engaged in covert operations against Iran. Fourth, respect means America needs to demonstrate empathy toward Iranians for what it and its friends and allies have done to Iran in the past. Fifth, respect means that as a state that is more powerful than Iran, the United States should make the first move to engage Iran." (10)

Also, three experts (Farideh Farhi from the University of Hawaii, George Perkovich of the Carnegie Endowment for International Peace and Cliff Kupchan of the Eurasia Group) have given response to a similar question.

"Margaret Warner: Let me go back to a phrase that both President Obama and President Ahmadenijad used in the early days of this administration - that they were ready for dialogue in an atmosphere of "mutual respect" - and they both used that phrase. And if we think about the atmospherics of this, what does that mean and - George Perkovich, starting with you - what does that mean in each country's case - mutual respect?

George Perkovich: Well, I think this is very important and I think it should be doable, especially in the U.S. side, to convey that kind of respect. And I think President Obama has begun to do that. But in particular, for the Iranian leadership - for the Iranian government - there's a sense that it's fair that - you know, the U.S. has never accepted the revolutionary government of Iran - the government that is - whose supreme leader is a religious figure, now Ayatollah Khamenei - the U.S. never conveys respect for that government but basically says that this is a government that is more or less, you know, illegitimate, should be changed, is not democratic, and so on.

Farideh Farhi: From the Iranian point of view, I think the parliament's speaker, Ali Larijani, speaking in Munich, used the language that the United States should stop boxing with us and start playing chess with us. And I think in terms of the dynamics of the current situation -the current talks - Iran is essentially beyond the general ideas about the United States accepting the Iranian Revolution and so on and is focused on the nature of the conversation.

Cliff Kupchan: just [coming] from my visits to Tehran, it really is striking - I think there's kind of a cultural factor here. Respect is something, almost in a Middle Eastern sense that Iran demands. When you ask Iranian leaders, well, what do you want? Do you want us to lift sanctions? Do you want security guarantees? The answer is, we want respect...I think approaching them as a legitimate country is the right way to go." (11)

What do I think?

I believe when the regime of Iran is talking about the "mutual respect", it has certain points in mind, which goes beyond what these scholars are thinking. The Iranian leaders have some far reaching points in mind. The code words of "mutual respect" contains not only grievances of Iran but also the security guarantees that the regime wants in addition to a free hand in matters that it considers as internal or regional or peculiar to Muslims or the Iranians (Shiites especially).

These are:

1- Do not interfere in our internal affairs.

2- Do not talk to us about human rights (issues such as women, students and press freedoms, NGOs, human right activists, the UN resolutions about condemnation of the violations of the human rights in Iran, the obligations of Iran as a state according to the Universal Declaration of Human Rights or the UN

Conventions on the Civil and Political or Economic and Social Rights)

3- Do not interfere in what we do under the pretext of religion (stoning of adulterers and gays, killing those who change their religion, assassination of opponents, killing, if necessary by terroristic tactics, those who humiliate Islam in our view and so on)

4- We do not need your democracy. Your democracy is the offspring of Christianity and Judeo-Christian culture, and Anglo-Saxon history and Western liberalism. We have an Islamic theocracy based on Shiite-Islamic views of our regime (no matter that many do not consider the existing ideology in Iran as Islamic or even Shiite) and it has nothing to do with you, even when it says that you are the enemies. In return, we do nothing. What? Nothing? Yes, nothing, because we were not doing anything bad to begin with.

Notes:

(1) http://rajanews.com, "complete text of Iran's proposed package to the 5+1", 09/12/2009 in Persian

(2) http://www.realclearpolitics.com/articles/2009/03/obama_nowruz_message_to_iran.html

(3) http://www.sindhtoday.net/world/61615.htm

(4) ISNA

(5) http://www.mohammadmossadegh.com/news/iran-to-obama-show-us-the-change

(6) http://www.mohammadmossadegh.com/news/iran-to-obama-show-us-the-change

(7) http://www.aryanews.com/Default.aspx?cod=1020081011001285, in Persian

(8) http://shahabnews.com/prtjaiev.uqevmzsffu.html, 02/07/2009

(9) http://www.kayhannews.ir/Detail.aspx?cid=7626 No. 19304, 29th of Bahman 1387

(10) http://www.niacouncil.org/index.php?option=com_content &task=view&id=1332&Itemid=29, 5 Feb. 2009

(11) http://www.pbs.org/newshour/insider/middle_east/jan-june09/iran_02-17.html)

Mass Murder of 1988 in Iran: Iranian Killing Fields

It was the end of Iran-Iraq war (1980-1988) and I was sent to Evin Prison for an indefinite time. The agent of the Intelligence Ministry who was escorting me to the prison let me lift my eye-cover and look around. He said: you are not going to leave this place alive, so have a look.

In those days, eye-cover was an essential part of the prison attire and no prisoner was allowed to be without it. The Evin Prison was a beautiful place in the foothills of Alborz Mountain in north Tehran. It had been turned into a security prison at the time of the Shah, but the Islamic Government had turned it into an independent unit. Evin had everything inside it: the revolutionary court, office of the revolutionary prosecutor, the solitary cells, public prison, and office of the Intelligence Ministry, women' section, execution chambers and even the clergies' ward.

I was thinking that the prison must be overcrowded because so many people were arrested those days and taken there. However, I came to know that the prison was almost empty. The few prisoners who had remained acted as zombies. They did not show any interest in talking to anyone. It took a while to know that the judicial and prison officials had killed several thousand prisoners within a few days. During the several years that I spent there, I came to know many parts of this issue little by little, but I was always surprised why the people and organizations outside of prison, inside and outside of Iran, did not at all talk about such a horrible mass murder. Later, when I had a meeting with the Representative of the UN Human Rights Commission (Dr. Galindo Pohl), as one of the prisoners who had been interviewed by the UN Delegation, I was surprised that even he did not ask me or any other prisoner (as far as I know after talking to the persons that I knew) about this case.

What happened was that at the end of Iran-Iraq war, while Iran had accepted the UNSC 598 Resolution to end the war, the forces of the MKOs (Mujahedin Khalgh Organization) were staging an attack from the Iraqi borders. The Iranian army was pushed back by Iraqis who were using chemical weapons on a large scale and the tactic of human waves of the Iranian military leaders had failed. Khomeini had "drunk the chalice of poison" and if the Americans did not stop the Iraqi army, Saddam intended to recapture all territories that he had got at the beginning of the 8 year war. Out of the fear of the collapse of the regime, the so called Founder of the Islamic Republic, Mullah Khomeini, ordered all prisoners in Evin and a couple of other security prisons (like Kachoi Prison in Karaj) to be asked one question: "do you insist on your positions?" Whoever answered in a way that indicated that he or she had not repented was sentenced to immediate execution.

The mass killings were conducted under the supervision of several persons: Lajevardi, the Head of Evin Prison, Mullah Naieri in the revolutionary court, Mullah Niazi in the office of the prosecutor. They were highly rewarded later: Lajevardi (the Bucher of Evin) became the Head of the Prisons Organization of Iran; Mullah Nairi became the Head of Center for Execution of Imam's Instructions (this is one of the less known organizations in Iran which controls most of the properties of the wealthy people from the time of Shah that have been confiscated. It has huge assets all over Iran and it makes considerable contributions to Mullahs that follow the orders of the so-called Supreme Leader), and Mullah Niazi became the Head of the State Inspectorate Organization.

The Mullahs that were issuing death sentences were flying by helicopter from one prison to another every day and asking the only question that was on the table. I heard between 3 and 8 thousand prisoners were mass murdered. Most of the prisoners that were killed belonged to the MKOs. The majority of the rest belonged to the leftist organizations like Paykar, the Fadayian (Minority), and Rahe-Kargar. I think the fact that the majority of the prisoners killed were MKOs and leftist groups played an important role in ignoring the Iranian version of the Killing Fields.

The prisoners that were chosen for the immediate execution were in different stages of their judicial proceedings or sentences. There were people who had served their sentences or those who had never been to a court. The executioners had a hard time handling the huge killing spree. The prisoners were executed by hanging in the chambers where tens of ropes were fastened to several pipes in the ceiling (I saw personally the inside of an execution chamber).

They used also firing squads. The murdered prisoners were carried by big trucks and dumped in a place outside of Tehran in an area called Khavaran, in the mass graves that were unmarked. The relatives of the prisoners were left uniformed and those who somehow came to know the reality were not allowed to have any public mourning ceremony.

This issue is one of the most obvious cases of crimes against humanity, violation of human rights, and criminal acts of the Islamic regime of Iran and on the anniversary of the mass killings, it deserves to be mentioned extensively.

IRAN, HOLOCAUST AND AHMADINEJAD

I ran has been a home for the Jewish people in the course of history. Cyrus the Great, the Iranian king, freed the Jews from the prisons of Babylon after taking over this area almost 2500 years ago. He helped the Jews to go back to their lands in Jerusalem. His name has been mentioned in the Old Testament repeatedly as a savior of the Jewish people.

During the Second World War, an Iranian named Sardari who was the Charge of the Iranian Embassy in Paris acted as the Iranian version of Schindler (the person who was the subject of the movie Schindler's List), he made serious correspondence with the Nazi authorities that had occupied France and argued that Iranian Jews were of a special race as compared to the others and they were in fact:" Mousavi" Jews. He managed to save the lives of an unknown number of people.

Under these circumstances, the present regime of Iran is holding the Holocaust conference in Iran in order to cast doubt on the validity of the incident.

Why? What does Iran have to gain?

The remarks of the Iranian president Ahmadinejad, makes Iran look like a country having deep interests and affections about the issue of Palestine and Israel. The reality is that most of the Iranians do not know where Palestine is and almost all of Iranians do not care what has happened to the Palestinians. Then, how come the leaders of the Islamic Republic of Iran, starting from Khomeini and reaching the current president of Iran, keep talking about the issue of Palestine as if it is the first priority for Iran? The answer is very clear. Attending the problems of Iran through inefficient and demagogue managers is not possible, but it is easy to talk about the Palestinians.

After 30 years of Islamic propaganda and choosing some days as the days for commemoration of the Palestinian issues, paying billions of dollars to the Palestinians, selling cheap and even giving free oil to the crooks governing Syria for supporting the same groups of the Palestinians, after building thousands of meaningless statues, and other things for Ghods (the Dome of Rock) and naming the streets of Iran with Arabic names, and bringing the Palestinians to Iran for hospitalization, paying rewards to the suicide killers and other acts, the Iranians are as alien to the issues of Palestine as they have ever been. Perhaps some section of the Iranians had a kind of feeling for the Palestinians in the past, but now they are lost also.

Iranians have no interest in the fate of Palestine as long as their own fate is under question through the irresponsible and illogical acts of the leaders of the Islamic Republic of Iran. Iranians are not satisfied that even one cent of their money is spent for the supporting the cause or well-being of the Arab Palestinians as long as a third of the Iranian population lives under the poverty line. The Iranians do not care what happens to the Palestinians as long as Iranian rights are not respected and recognized by any Arab country. The Arabs have always threatened Iran. Among the Iranian neighbors, Iraq had always problems with Iran. Iran and Iraq were on the verge of fighting at the time of Shah. The only thing that stopped the Iraqis was the powerful army of Iran. The Islamic Republic fought with Iraq for 8 years, it is sure that the future government of Iraq will still be ready to fight Iran as soon as it gets the power.

During the last several months that the new president of the Islamic Republic of Iran was put in the post of presidency by the circles of power and through rigged elections, he has spoken more about the issues related to Palestine than Iran which makes some people wonder whether or not he is the president of Palestine. The hallucinating president of Iran has started to renew some of the old points about Palestine as if he has invented them.

WHO WAS THE WINNER:
IRAN OR THE USA?

(Translation of article and comments on it)

Two weeks after Mohammad Reza Shah entered New York for medical treatment, and exactly three days after the negotiations in Algiers between Engineer Bazarghan, Dr. Ebrahim Yazdi and Mostafa Chamran with Zbigniew Brezezinski, Carter's National Security Adviser, Tehran was ready to give birth to one of the most important events in its political history.

Four hundred students and the people, who were marching towards Tehran University since ten o'clock in the morning to protest the US policies, suddenly changed their course and entered the American Embassy. They took 72 persons out of the embassy staff as hostage and captured the embassy. This was in fact the second time since the victory of the Iranian Islamic Revolution in 1979 that the American embassy in Tehran was taken over. In February of the same year, almost 150 persons who belonged to the leftist forces and a group called "Fadaian Khalgh Guerrillas", who were convinced that the documents of SAVAK [Shah's secret police] had been transferred to the US embassy, and instigated by articles appearing in a newspaper in Baku [the Capital of Azerbaijan Republic, which was then still a part of the USSR], attacked the US Embassy. This incident was settled by good offices of the figures like Martyre Beheshti.

Why one year after the Islamic Revolution's victory in 1979, the US Embassy in Tehran, as an important strategic place, and near the Saudi Arabia, the important economic base of special importance for the USA, and as the gendarmes of the region, was attacked twice? At the same time, why the embassies of states like the UK and the USSR that had not been less harmful than the USA in damaging the course of politics, economics and culture of Iran in the past, were not attacked? These need a separate review. The main target of this piece is a new review of the reasons of the occupation of the US Embassy in Tehran and the events that followed it, including the sanctions against Iran, the Tabas attack [Hostage rescue operation], and the Imposed War [i.e. the Iran-Iraq war of 1980-88].

The popular uprising of the people of Iran, who had lived a long time under cruelty and sufferings of colonialism and its lackeys, eventually led to the ousting of and cutting of the Western dominance over Iran, especially by the USA, as the main source of the planning for Iran. The military and civilian advisers [of the USA] were deported from Iran. Now, all secret and open activities of the USA were concentrated in the US Embassy in Iran. According to the existing documents, many of which had been destroyed on November 4 and prior to that date, the most important duty of the US Embassy was trying to get in touch with the revolutionary elements and guiding them in the line of damaging the character of Imam Khomeini.

The most important reason for occupation of the US Embassy by the students was related to the events that happened in the year following the revolution. The two states had diplomatic relations. The Americans accepted the Shah who had fled from Iran and disregarded the requests of the Iranian officials for his extradition in order to stand trial. Imam Khomeini had issued a statement in the same field one day before the occupation of the embassy. Addressing all layers of the Iranian people, he said, "Academicians, university students and the students of the religious schools must enhance their combat against the USA in every possible means." Following this message, the group of students, called the Students Following the Line of Imam' and composed of students from the Tehran University, Shahid Beheshti, Sharif Industrial University, and Amir Kabir University attacked the US Embassy and occupied it.

Among the achievements of Iran from the occupation of the US Embassy, two cases are prominent: first, the myth of American power in the region was crushed. Iran turned into the dominant power in the region and later the voice of Iranian people and their protests was spread to the world. One of the first statements of the students occupying the embassy had noted "we, the Muslim students that follow the line of Imam, support the clear position of Imam against the criminal USA and in order to protest to the plots of imperialism and Zionism, have occupied the espionage embassy of the USA in Tehran and we intend to get our voice of protest to the hears of the people all over the world."

It should be noted that His Excellency the Imam, supported the occupation of the US Embassy by the students and called this action "a second revolution". He said, "Iran has a new revolution today. This is a revolution even bigger than the first one. This one is about the Great Satan, the USA."

The hostage-taking incident affected the internal politics in a surprising way. It affected the USA in particular. In the up-coming US elections in 1980, Carter failed to get the popular vote and Ronald Regan replaced him as the US President. This was an earthquake. An apparently small incident had happened in one of the countries that were long considered as the obedient slaves of the USA. Spiegel reported at the same time, "once the USA could decide who gets the seat of power in Iran. Now, in 1980, an Ayatollah in Tehran determines the outcome of the US Presidential elections." This was true indeed.

One of the special features of the occupation of the US Embassy was that the students, who did this move, were free-minded and they did not belong to any political line. Apart from the Imam, no administration, Majles official or any organization was influential in the decisions of the students. In several cases, there were struggles to get credits for certain political factions but they all failed and the healthiness of the incident was preserved until the last stage.

Gary Sick has referred in his book of memoirs to the meeting of Sadegh Ghotbzadeh, the then Iran's Foreign Minister, with Hamilton Jordan, the White House Chief of Staff, in Paris on 28th of Bahman [17th of February]. He has recorded, "after a three-hour meeting that was held secretly, Ghotbzadeh proposed a solution to Jordan and said: it is very easy to solve this crisis. Just kill the Shah." This is an example of the acute weakness and backwardness of the leading officials of the 'interim government" [of PM Mehdi Bazarghan]. They had failed to convince the students to act as they desired, and therefore they were trying to wipe out the details of the problem without solving it. Bani Sadr [the first Iranian president], in his first interview after he got the post of presidency, protected to the independence of the students [occupying the US Embassy] and said: " we have two governments in Iran: The government of the students following the line of Imam and the government headed by the Council of Revolution. This is not acceptable."

Another prominent characteristic of the incident, was the reaction of the international community and their unified stand in order to crush the spontaneous action of the Iranian combatants and force the students to stop the occupation of the embassy and release the hostages as quick as possible, which could be the best remedy to restore the lost prestige of the USA in the international community. This point was so important that Kurt Valdheim, the then UN Secretary General, declared that despite the refusal of the Iranian officials to invite him, he was determined to travel to Iran. Eventually no Iranian official welcomed him upon the arrival and he left Tehran after three days without any progress.

Although at the same time, the United Nations Security Council was deeply involved in the struggle and competition of the Eastern and Western Blocks headed by the USSR and the USA, and it had already lost its original aims, the US succeeded to get the approval of the USSR in the early days of the embassy incident and the members of the UN Security Council unanimously signed a declaration for condemning the hostage-taking in the embassy.

However, after this stage and the deepening of the incident and emergence of crisis in the extra-regional policy of the USA, the UNSC decided to adopt a resolution. The rivalry of the states, especially the USSR and the USA, which had renewed their old hostility, postponed the adoption of the resolution in the UNSC. Eventually, on 13th of January 1980, the UNSC held a meeting and under the U.S. pressure adopted a resolution against Iran. This resolution was faced with the Veto of the USSR and was sent to the cold files of the UNSC.

However, the USA declared that it was going to impose the sanctions unilaterally. The US did so, billions of dollars of the military, civilian and diplomatic assets of Iran were blocked, and the Iranians residing in the USA faced many hurdles and prosecutions. Many of them were deported and the US government imposed widespread economic sanctions against Iran.

Although these sanctions damaged seriously the Iranian economy, but due to the blow, which was stricken against the USA and the prestige that Iran had gained in the international community, actually it did not have any effect on the decisions of the officials and those who had planned this incident.

According to Carter, the then US President, the American politicians and decision makers of the US foreign policy has basically two line of dealing with this incident in mind:

1- Persons like Cyrus Vance, the then US Secretary of State, supported the diplomatic actions and dialogue and eventually a form of flight or economic sanctions against Iran. After the Hostage Rescue Operations in Tabas, he resigned.

2- Brezezinski, the National Security Adviser of Carter, advocated the military intervention and war operations as the best way to tackle the issue.

After the failure of the Tabas operations and the discussions that followed it, it was oblivious that dialogue was the only option left for the USA.

On the 4th of Farvardin[24th of March], Carter wrote a confidential letter to Imam Khomeini and mentioned: " we are ready to accept the new realities that have emerged out of the Iranian revolution. This is a constant aim for us. I believe that both of us are following the same aim, which is the universal peace and justice for all nations."

Imam ordered the public release of this confidential letter and a political fiasco was created for Carter.

When the USA failed to get its aims through carrots and sticks and using its internal elements, they asked the third parties to enter the scene and eventually the Algiers Declaration was concluded. According to the accords, the US was committed:

1- stop intervening in the internal affairs of Iran

2- abolish the sanctions imposed against Iran after 14th of November 1979

3- help to confiscate and return the assets of the Pahlavi Dynasty and their relatives in the USA

4- stop the filing suits against Iran due to the occupation of the embassy

5- The civil suites of the American citizens are referred to a mutually agreed arbitration tribunal.

In lieu of these, and after gradual implementation of the American commitments, Iran was committed to release the hostages.

In spite of all commitments, the US transferred a part of Iran's assets to an escrow account in the UK and stopped observing the other commitments. However, due to the good offices of friendly states, and the wining cards gained by Iran, the most important of which was cutting the hand of the USA and showing the power of the new revolution in Iran to the world, after 444 days, 52 remaining hostages were sent first to Algiers and then to their state.

The 444 days of hostage taking must be considered as one of the most important and crucial incidents in the post-revolutionary Iran. This is reflected in the words Imam: "this was a revolution, bigger than the first one." The Iranian revolution, like many popular movements in the world, could return to the old ways under the social and political conditions. The revolutions that have happened in the South America were an oblivious example of this point. However, the hostage-taking incident, in a short while after the revolution in Iran, revealed the lines of hostility and the plots that were hatched in secret. It helped to explain the positions of Iran in the international community and made the conditions of Iran for relations with other states of the world very clear.

NOTES OF THE TRANSLATOR

1- The Hostage-taking in the US Embassy in Tehran was an action against the International law, the national interests of Iran and even against Islam. For more information in this line , please refer to: R. K. Ramazani, Iran's Hostage Crisis: International Legitimacy Matters, Comparative Studies of South Asia, Africa and the Middle East, Duke University Press, Vol. 25, No.2, 2005, pp. 273-278.

2- Some of the problems created for Iran due to this incident are as follows:

i- Isolation of Iran in the international community

j- The loss of possible positive reaction of the US officials towards the new regime.

k- Stopping of the Iran-US relations

l- Start of an artificial stage in the US-Iran relations. In one side, the government of the Islamic Republic insisted on the hostility towards the USA, and on the other side, the people of Iran loved the USA.

m- Gradual inclination of the USA to confront the regime of Iran

n- Creation of a wall of distrust between two states

o- Comparative support of the Iraqis in the Iran-Iraq war (1980-88) p- Discrediting Iran in international forums like the UNSC and ICJ (it condemned Iran for violation of the Vienna Conventions on Diplomatic and Consular Relations). The result was that the UNSC waited 6 years before issuing its first resolution about the Iran-Iraq war.

3- Most of the persons that formed the so-called students following the line of Imam that took over the US Embassy in Tehran were not students. There were active members of the MKOs, the Leftist Marxist-Leninist Group of Fadaian Khalgh, and the Communist Tudeh party of Iran among them. As it appears in the above article, these groups had practiced the takeover of the embassy in another occasion.

4- It is clear from the above article and many other sources, including the book published by Massomeh Ebtekar, that the students were acting in a professional way. In her book, Takeover in Tehran: the inside story of the 1979 US Embassy Capture, Canada, Talonbooks, 2000, Ebtekar, who was known as " Mary' to the journalists that covered the incident and she translated the for the hostage-takers, tries to give the impression that she was not a member of the hostage takers. In fact she was a hostage-taker. Her husband (Hashemi) was also one of the hostage takers. She was awarded for her role in this incident later by getting a scholarship from Iranian government to get PhD in a western university and became the Deputy President and Head of the Iranian Environment Protection Organization.

5- Some of the so-called students of the line of Imam were rewarded later by becoming prominent officials in the Iranian oil ministry. Also a number of them became high ranking officials, and ambassadors of the Iranian foreign ministry. Mr. Shiekholislam, who was a long time the Deputy Foreign Minister of Iran in Political affairs, during the tenure of Dr. Velayati, was one of the leaders of the so-called students.

6- The takeover of the embassy was not an instantaneous act at all. The criminals that did this action had planned everything before. They had communications devices that belonged to the law-enforcement official and they were armed. The attackers well aware (probably by listening to the telephone calls of the

US Embassy) that the Charge D'affair and two other officials of the American Embassy were out of the Embassy and they were waiting for them to return. Eventually when it was clear that the three diplomats were not returning so soon, they went ahead and attacked the Embassy.

7- Khomeini had provoked the people to act against the USA, but he did not know about the plan to attack the US Embassy. First, he asked his foreign minister, Dr. Ebrahim Yazdi (according to the interviews of Yazdi with the Iranian media on the occasion of the anniversary of the embassy takeover), to go and throw out the students, but later the students (and the leftist agents) convinced Khomeini that he could use the existing documents (or documents that did not exist, but he could claim that they have it) to discredit his opponents. Khomeini, who the master of mounting the waves (he had gained experience through stealing the Iranian revolution), accepted to support the move. In one case (the case of Engineer Abbas Amir Entezam, the Spokesperson of the Interim Government of Iran, who was later arrested and put to prison for espionage and he is still there after 27 years), the students showed a letter from the US Embassy addressed to Amir Entezam that has started with "Dear Sir" and they argued that Amir Entezam was so close to the Americans that they called him "Dear Sir". It is interesting that years later, when some of the so-called Students of the Line of Imam started to act a little different from the official line (some of them supported the relations with the USA, some said that they regretted that were part of this action and others appeared as supporters of reforms), they were tried and imprisoned by the same methods and criteria. Abbas Abdi, one of the leading hostage takers, had formed a kind of Think Tank and he performed a public opinion poll in Iran couple years ago. He reached the conclusion that a great majority of Iranian want good relations with the USA. He and his close associates were immediately arrested and charged with espionage. It took no time for a few of his colleagues to "remember" that they were US spies in Iran and they confessed and apologized for that.

(1) Http;//www.baztab.ir/news/52218.php, dated 11/04/2006. The article is written in Farsi by Mehdi Salimi

Iran's Evin Prison and Its Butcher, Asadollah Lajevardi

Evin was originally a village in the suburbs of Tehran. The entire village apparently belonged to Sayed Ziaeddin Tabatabai, the first Prime Minister of Iran after the 1921 coup d'état of Reza Khan, who later assumed the throne as Reza Shah. Thus, many parts of Evin bore the name of Sayed Ziaeddin Tabatabai.

In fact, the big plot of land next to Evin Prison is called Sayed Zia's Garden. Apparently, a few years before I went to Evin (serving a sentence there from 1988 to 1996), the personnel of Evin had asked for and received permission from Khomeini to build themselves a housing complex in Sayed Zia's Garden. Asadollah Lajevardi, the notorious head of Evin Prison, used the services of a crook named Reza Zavareie, his friend in the Mafia known as the Coalition of Islamic Societies (Hayate Motalefeh Eslami) who had become the head of Iran's Properties Registration Organization , to seize ownership of the concerned garden.

Eventually, Lajeverdi established a complex there called "garden of paradise" (*Dashte behesht*). The place was turned into a big partying center for the zealots of the regime during Lajevardi's tenure as head of the prison. High-ranking regime officials, wealthy bazaaris (the financial backbone of the mullahs), and the nouveaux riches among the clerics were using the premises for ceremonies for marriage and Hajj. They paid Lajevardi a great deal of money for the privilege.

This was one of the reasons that the personnel of Evin Prison hated Lajevardi. They were so angry at this act that many of them cursed him openly in their conversations. I personally heard one of them praying for his assassination. Lajevardi was, of course, assassinated in 1998 (by MKO members, it is said), after having left the Prisons Organization and gone back to the bazaar for a new kind of plundering.

A part of the village of Evin was devoted to Evin Prison during the time of Mohammad Reza Shah. It was intended as a place for tackling political and security prisoners. A number of political anti-Shah activists were killed, tortured or incarcerated in Evin. In fact, the notoriety of Evin Prison had its roots in the Shah's time, though it did not see its darkest days until the atrocities after the establishment of the Islamic Republic of Iran through the plots of the mullahs. Evin was a complex at the time of the Shah, housing a special unit of the Imperial Guard as well as a section run by SAVAK, the Shah's secret police. When people captured Evin during the revolution (1979), all sorts of rumors were circulating that Evin had secret chambers and underground wards, but no one found any such thing. Evin Prison is in the northwest of Tehran, on the street named after the prison. Before arriving at the prison gate one reaches a sharp slope near an intersection famously called the "slope of destiny" (*sarashib-e sarnevesht*). This always reminded me of the Bab al-Mandab ("gateway of lamentation"), the strait separating Djibouti in Africa from Yemen in Asia. It is said that captured black slaves wept when they passed the strait, because they knew it was the point of no return and they were never going to see their homeland again.

When I saw Evin, it was several years after the revolution. It had everything: solitary confinement, a public ward, closed-door rooms, and sections for the intelligence ministry, office of the Prisons Organization, office of the prosecutor general, and execution chambers.

Lajevardi and his friends had turned Evin into a self-sufficient unit. After the main gate of Evin, on the right were buildings housing the Islamic Republic's office for the revolutionary prosecutor general. Later, when I worked in the prison premises, I came to know that the execution chamber was also next to the building of the prosecutor general. On the left were the buildings of the Islamic Revolutionary Courts, which resembled an apartment complex. The office of the Prisons Organization was further down on the left.

The office of Evin Prison was a small building on the right. People sat there waiting for the guards to send them to the different sections of the prison. They could be newcomers or those who had returned from the courts, the interrogation chambers or the office of the prosecutor general.

The first time I was in the prison office, blindfolded and accompanied by a group of others sitting there all facing the wall and with blindfolds, someone shouted: "Learning center (*amuzeshgah*), sanatorium (*asayeshgah*)." I did not move because I thought this did not apply to me. After a few seconds a guard came to me and said: "Hey, move! You are going to the sanatorium." I found out later that they had divided the prison into these two sections: "sanatorium" really meant solitary confinement, and "learning center" was the public section of the prison.

These two units, along with the workshops of Evin, were in the foothills of the Alborz mountain range, and several minibuses carried people to and from those sections. The windows of the minibuses were painted over, but looking carefully from under the blindfold and though the small openings in the covering of windows, one could see that the premises were a big garden with enormous trees.

These arrangements of the sections had a special meaning. The prison authorities considered the prison as a place for repentance of the ignorant and the deceived. They thought people who came to prison would first have a chance to "rest" in solitary confinement and then be "re-educated" in prison.

Those who were impervious to re-education at any stage of their stay were sent to the execution chambers immediately. This was an attempt to comply with an ambiguous utterance by Khomeini written in very large letters over the main buildings of Evin: "Prison must be a university." I conducted research about this later and found it was a misinterpretation of Khomeini's sentences as usual. (Khomeini used the Persian language more like a foreigner than a native speaker. Unlike the usual practice of putting verbs at the end of the sentence, for instance, he used the verbs at the beginning.)

The public ward in Evin was in fact the offices and living quarters and facilities of the Shah's guards. The converted tailoring workshop had been the swimming pool of the previous guards. The solitary confinement complex had new and old sections. It was four floors. The last floor was devoted to the mentally retarded prisoners and it was an extremely horrible section.

The lowest level was devoted to women, but the main women's ward was somewhere close to the main offices. The office of the ministry of intelligence, called 209, was also attached to those sections. I was a constant customer of this office along with almost thirty other people.

Some of the prisoners, especially the younger MKO members, had turned into prison trustees and were called *tawwab*s ("penitents"). They treated the others very badly. I think the reason was that by the time we reached Evin, a great number of the MKO members had been killed and the remaining ones felt they had to prove their "repentance."

Lajevardi was one of the persons that had a special place in hell. He was one of the most hated men that I came to know in my life. He was a corrupt, hypocritical, and violent creature. The ugliness of his face—a personification of Satan in my mind—added to his repulsive personality. When I entered Evin Prison, he was already the Head of Prisons Organization of Iran. Lajevardi belonged to the Coalition of Islamic Groups (Hay'at-e Motalefeh Eslami), the religious terrorist group that had assassinated Hassanali Mansour, the PM of the Shah, and was related

to the Muslim Brotherhood in Arab countries through a few traitors to the Iranian nation. The Coalition of Islamic Groups still
plays a Mafiosi role in the government and politics of the Islamic
Republic of Iran, and some of its important figures are: Asgaro-
ladi, Khamenei (the so-called Supreme Leader), Ayatollah Yazdi,
then the head of Judiciary but virtually Lajevardi's puppet, and
Zavareie (d. 2005), the head of the Office for Property Registration that helped Lajevardi in his corrupt activities.

Lajevardi spent a great deal of time in Evin. He was instrumental
in all the killings there after the so-called revolution. He worked
there as interrogator, torturer, executioner, head of branch, head
of prison and, finally, head of Prisons Organization, which was
inside Evin. He considered Evin his child.

Other than a few persons who were isolated, he had gathered a
bunch of idiots to run Evin. Anyone who began to suspect corruption within the management of the prison was sacked right
away. Some were sent to the cells of Evin as soon as they raised
a protest. Lajevardi was very fond of the landscape in Evin. For
him the beauty of Evin as a garden was very important, even
more important than the prisoners and prison staff. For the same
reason both groups hated him.

Another thing that made Lajevardi very disgusting was his deep
hypocrisy. He used to punish the prisons and prison personnel
for trivial things while he and his family were plundering in the
millions from the public treasury. Once he inflicted severe punishment on a person employee because he washed his car inside
Evin with public water. Evin has great workshops. In the tailoring workshop alone, more than a thousand industrial sewing
machines were working several shifts.

Lajevardi confiscated what these workshops produced and hauled
it away in a big trailer. A prisoner who was a friend of mine managed the accounting for the tailoring workshop. He told me personally how he had to alter names and cook the books to conceal
the stealing. At that time Lajevardi's son-in-law and father-in-law
both were working in the management of the workshop. Later,
when the thieves reached a point of conflict over the division of

the spoils, Lajevardi put some of his family in prison for corruption. They had been working there for more than fifteen years and Lajevardi claimed he did not know the scope of corruption.

Lajevardi was also a symbol of mismanagement in the Islamic Republic of Iran. He had been a petty tradesman in bazaar, and when he had reached high places in the system he was still thinking of management in terms of running a small bazaar stall (*hojreh*). Combined with mismanagement was a general sickness of nature that he shared with other managers in the Islamic Republic at all levels, from the head of sweepers in a small region all the way up to the Supreme Leader. This sickness of mind derives from a deep conviction that God has given a special and unique talent and power of decision-making to a select few and whatever comes to their miserable minds is the best thing that can be done.

This kind of thinking resulted in untold disasters in Evin and other prisons in Iran during the tenure of Lajevardi. Among other things, Lajevardi arbitrarily and illegally changed regulations and procedures in prison management, and he mixed prisoners of various types to conceal political prisoners.

The changing of the prison bylaws (*ayin-nameh zendanha*) was egregiously illegal. It made his task easier that the laws and regulations of the Islamic Republic of Iran, starting with the Constitution and going down to ordinary statutes, are replete with mistakes, points of injustice, contraventions of Islamic jurisprudence, violations of the Universal Declaration of Human Rights, and even contrary to common sense. The new prison bylaws that Lajevardi cooked up contradicted even to the miserable laws of the Islamic Republic of Iran.

Lajevardi had ordered Ayatollah Yazdi, his protégé and scarecrow in the judiciary of Iran for many years, to sign the new prison bylaws without so much as reading a single line. Bylaws clearly should go through a process to become enforceable. Usually, such important bylaws must go through the appropriate parliamentary committees and come to a full vote on the floor of the parliament, then go through the government apparatus like the council of ministers, and so on. The new prison bylaws never went through those steps; only the chief of the Judiciary put his signature to them, which in no way invests them with legal authority.

Other problems that I remember with the new bylaws are as follows:

1. In the classification of prisoners there was no distinction between criminal and political prisoners.

2. Prisoners that were called "spies" and "criminals against the security of the country" (which encompassed all non-ordinary criminals) were deprived of almost all advantages in prison.

3. According to new articles in the bylaws, a prisoner who learned a part of the Koran by heart became eligible for a few days' furlough. This was a ridiculous chapter in prison life. Many of the intellectual prisoners who refused were denied privileges, while hard-core criminals who learned small parts of the Koran without knowing what it meant could spend time outside prison. Numerous reports indicated that these furloughed prisoners stole cars right within the prison neighborhood, raped women, drank heavily and engaged in disorderly conduct, and even committed murder.

4. Limiting the power of judges over the prisoners as opposed to the powers of prison officials. This may look like an innocent provision, deceptively so. For many years, starting with the first days of the revolution, the judges of the Revolutionary Courts handed out sentences to their victims (political and ideological prisoners) with no clear criteria. They had sent many to their deaths, and those who were not killed were supposed to be ready for some kind of rehabilitation. Therefore, the judges granted furloughs, or even released the prisoners when they were convinced that they were no longer a threat to the regime. Contrary to that, if someone the

judges considered a threat to the regime had served out the full prison term, they refused to release him or her. Now, Lajevardi had changed the prison regulations to divest judges of decision-making in cases where they knew that the sentence was meant to be open-ended and conditioned on the behavior of the prisoner. A judge had given a 20-year sentence to someone who may have deserved a six-month prison according to ordinary laws, and now after two years he was convinced that the prisoner should go home, but Lajevardi and his bylaws would not allow it. The duration of furloughs for the prisoners was very limited, because Lajevardi wanted to keep people in prison and use them as slaves in the prison workshops, from which he derived considerable wealth. Political prisoners and prisoners of conscience—those for whom prison furloughs were actually devised—were denied their freedom entirely.

Pishva

This was the name given to a miserable, illiterate man. Lajevardi quickly discovered his violent character and wide-scale idiocy. He had become the head of Evin Prison during the time that I was in a cell there. The appointment of Pishva was ridiculous, because everybody knew that Lajevardi would not give up his dear child, Evin Prison. Pishva's real name was Karbalai, but most called him Hitler. Almost all the personnel of Evin and the revolutionary courts had pseudonyms, while prisoners and their families had given them special names. For instance, the man that prison officials called Haj Hussein was known to the prison population as Hussein the "honorless" (*bi-namus*). Prisoners referred to another character as "Hassan Zapata," because he had Mexican features.

Lajevardi devised a plan for Evin Prison that cost him his job, and eventually his life. To bolster the claim that Evin did not contain political prisoners, he opened the prison to dangerous criminals. The staff and administration of Evin were accustomed to political prisoners and did not know the ways of felons. The newcomers had no fear of the prison guards, who were ill-equipped to deal with them. These dangerous murderers, thieves or prostitutes assumed the most pious appearances, denying the guards the tool of branding them as irreligious or regime opponents. The customary threats Evin guards had used against political prisoners (whereby those that did not "behave" could travel the distance between life and death very quickly) had little effect on these dangerous criminals. Unlike the political prisoners who had almost never attempted an escape, the hardened felons made numerous attempts, succeeding in some cases. Some of them threatened the family of the guards out of the prison. During my time in Evin, I was aware of at least two cases where the prisoners had brazenly robbed the house of the head of the public section and other Evin officials. These dangerous prisoners were not processed by revolutionary courts, which did not know or follow the intricacies of the legal system. As a result, these felons did not fear the lawlessness of these courts. Some of them were rich and could buy the services of low-level workers who served as guards in the prison. Unlike the political prisoners, who showed no interest in corrupt actions, the criminals took advantage of the ignorance and incompetence of the Evin staff to engage in corruption within jail.

What is "Islamo-fascism"?

Islamo-fascism is a new name but the concept has a long history. It is clearly a combination between the ways of looking at Islam, with the policies of the fascist regimes of the twentieth century in Europe. (1) Although there are serious discussions about the exact meaning and extent of fascism (2), and the roots of the term (3) most of the sources agree that some characteristics are common in all fascist regimes such as:

1-Love of war and the acute need for foreign enemies that can be accused of all shortcomings

2- Military rule

3- Lack of tolerance and respect for other ideologies

4- Disregard of human rights

5- Authoritarian or totalitarian regime

6- Demagogic tactics to rally the support of people

7- Using zealots and paid lackeys for putting pressure and even elimination of opponents

8- Claiming to have a divine mission

9- The arrogance of believing in the superiority of one particular ideology (their own) over all others.

We can find all of these characteristics in the regime of the Islamic Republic of Iran:

1- Love of war: There is no limit in fighting against the infidels in the ideology of the ruling regime in Iran. There is no distinction between the military and civilian population. Every person of the un-Islamic world is an enemy.

The people are divided into us and them. Even the Muslims if they do not cooperate with the regime of Iran are considered as "them". Mullah Khomeini, the so-called founder of the Islamic Republic in Iran, always called the Iran-Iraq war (1980-1988) that resulted in killing of millions of people in Iran and Iraq and devastation of the two countries, a God given blessing. The administration of Iran under the presidency of Ahmadinejad claims to revive the legacy of Mullah Khomeini and for the same reason they are very interested in starting some kind of war in the region.

2- Military rule. The regime of Iran has been heavily relying on the military elements who are indoctrinated by the ruling Mullahs. The Islamic Revolutionary Guards used to have many sensitive posts in Iran and in the last two years or so (especially since the administration of Ahmadinejad was installed in Iran by the rigged elections), they have taken many civilian posts.

3- Lack of tolerance and respect for other ideologies- the regime of the Islamic Republic of Iran has been promoting religious intolerance. The freedom of expression for all groups has been violated and the mass media are under strict control of the regime. Under the new administration in Iran the extent of intolerance towards all religious and non-religious groups has increased.

4- Disregard of human rights- The principles of human rights as mentioned in the Universal Declaration of Human Rights and the UN Convention on the Civil and Political Rights and the Convention on Social and Economic Rights are all considered as tools of expansion of the Western cultures and they are rejected as such. Killing of the violators of the Islamic rules is permitted by God. Women are not equal to men. Democracy is void.

The population of the states, even in the Islamic states is not entitled to decide about their fate. The religious leaders decide what is good for the people. Arts, educational institutions, cultural activities, music, literature, painting, sculpturing, and so on must only be in the service of the Islamic tenets as defined by the religious authorities. There is no freedom of assembly, freedom of press and freedom of expression; the people rally in the streets when the officials say so and they demand whatever the religious leaders have defined.

Religious and other minorities are not supported and there is clear contradiction between Islam and the universal standards of human rights. Almost all 30 articles of the Universal Declaration of Human Rights are seriously violated by the Islamic Regime of Iran.

The most important cases are: the violation of women's rights (the regime of Iran is not ready to accept the equality of men and women and as such it has refused to adhere to the UN International Convention of the Elimination of all kinds of Discrimination Against Women), violation of the fundamental freedoms for the minorities in Iran (including the Baha'is), violation of the fundamental freedoms of the Iranian people, mistreatment of the political prisoners, and violating the rule of law.

5- Authoritarian or totalitarian regime- the regime of Iran is openly the enemy of democracy. The Mullahs of Iran have made it clear time and again that they do not believe in the role of people in determining their own destiny. Ayatollah Khazali, a prominent member of the Iranian Constitutional Assembly (Majles Khobreghan or Council of Islamic Experts) has said: "...what is the meaning of the people's demands? Who are the people to demand anything? The people should only implement the rules of Allah." (4) Also, Ayatollah Mesbah Yazdi, the Head of Imam Khomeini's Educational and Research Institute, has said: "... the legitimacy of the Supreme Leader comes from the infallible Imams, not from the people." (5) Khomeini had said: "...do not listen to those who speak about democracy. These are enemies of Islam. Anyone who wants a republic is our enemy did you create this revolution to become like Swiss? We break the poisonous pens of those who talk about nationalism, democracy and similar things..." Also, Dr. Ali Shariati, the great demagogue and fabricator of the Islamic hallucinations, and at the same time, the biggest ideological backbone of the Islamic Revolution in Iran has said: "leadership can't be the result of common people's votes. It can't come out of the corrupt masses of the people. Imam is directly responsible for the policy of the society and he has direct leadership in economy, army, culture, foreign and domestic policies..." He adds in another source (Shiitism, a comprehensive party): "It is necessary to have blind obedience. This is the real meaning of emulation in Shiitism. The same applies to the deputy of the Imam...a person that does not know his Imam, is like a sheep that has lost its Sheppard."

6- Demagogic tactics to rally the support of people- the street demonstrations have become the standard method of the Iranian Islamic regime to show the will and demands of the people. However, it is clear that no rally or demonstration is held in Iran unless all of its arrangements (including the slogans and the resolutions) are defined by the government. The staged demonstrations are manned by the groups that get special privileges from the regime and in many cases the demonstrators do not know the subject of demonstration before they get to the predetermined places.

7- Using zealots and paid lackeys for putting pressure and even elimination of opponents- the zealots who are trained to attack the opponents are an active part of the governmental apparatus of the Islamic regime in Iran. The religious thugs attack the gathering of the people, enter the houses and places of business and harass the people. They attack the speakers in the places if they are not approved by the regime and they attack women who have not observed the Islamic code of dress.

8- Claiming to have a divine mission- it is one of the most important features of the Islamic regime in Iran that it thinks it has a divine mission to change the world order. The followers of the Hidden Imam in Iran think that the Imam is going to appear and conquer the whole world and they should make themselves ready for war in the army of the Hidden Imam (6) The regime of the Islamic Republic of Iran believes that it has a divine mission to fight the Western culture and impose policies that it considers to be Islamic.

9- The arrogance of believing in the superiority of one particular ideology (their own) over all others- the regime of the Islamic Republic of Iran believes in the supremacy of the version of Islam practiced by the Iranian Mullahs as the best arrangement for the whole world. For the same reason, Ahmadinejad had asked President Bush to have a free televised discussion with him about which system (the Western liberalism or the Islamic regime as practiced in Iran) was good to be the world order. (7) The regime of the Islamic Republic of Iran believes that the Western way of life is corrupt. The regime of Iran is seriously thinking that the Western democracies are going to fall, as the USSR fell, and one of these days the Islamic regime will get a chance to introduce its role at the global level. It does not believe in validity of any arrangement with the "Western infidels" and all of the agreements with the West are temporary and subject to abrogation as soon as the Islamic power gets the opportunity to do so. The regime of the Islamic Republic of Iran believes that it needs to have nuclear weapons in order to manage the world. In fact, certain circles in Iran believe that when the Hidden Imam appears, the Imam would need weapons like nuclear weapons to implement his mission.

A look at the regime of Iran reveals that all of these elements are clearly present in the government and politics of the present regime of the Islamic Republic of Iran and it very much deserves to be included under the title of Islamofacist regimes.

Notes:

(1) http://en.wikipedia.org/wiki/Islamofascism

It is mentioned in this source that: "Islamofascism is neologism and political epithet used to induce an association of the ideological or operational characteristics of certain modern Islamist movements with European fascist movements of the early 20th century, neo-fascist movements, or totalitarianism.

Organizations that have been labeled "Islamofascist" include Al-Qaeda, the current government of Iran, the Taliban, Muslim Brotherhood, Hamas, and Hezbollah..."

(2) http://www.remember.org/his.root.what.html, dated 27 Sept. 1992. In this source, Chip Berlet describes: "...fascism and Nazism as ideologies, involve to varying degrees, some of the following hallmarks: 1- Nationalism and super-patriotism with a sense of historic mission. 2- Aggressive militarism even to the extent of glorifying war as good for the national or individual spirit. 3- Use of violence or threats of violence to impose views on others (fascism and Nazism both employed street violence and state violence at different moments in their development). 4- Authoritarian reliance on a leader or elite not constitutionally responsible to an electorate. 5- Cult of personality around charismatic leader. 6- Reaction against the values of modernism, usually with emotional attacks against both liberalism and communism. 7- Exhortations for the homogeneous masses of common folk... 8- Dehumanization and using the enemy as an scapegoat 9-The self image of being superior form of social organization beyond socialism, capitalism, and democracy..."

(3) http://www.opinionjournal.com/forms/printThis. html?id=110000882, dated 20 August 2006. In this source, Roger Scruton has mentioned: "...the term Islamofascism was introduced by the French writer Maxine Rodinson (1915-2004) to describe the Iranian revolution of 1978. The word has therefore caught on, not least because it provides a

convenient way of announcing that you are not against Islam, but only against its perversion by the terrorists...."

(4) http://www.iranian.com/News/2000/June/khaz.html, dated 08/27/2006, speaking for the congregational prayer.

(5) http://news.gooya.com/politics/archieves/2006/09/052663print. php, dated 09/10/2006

(6) The role of Hidden Imam in the history and politics of the Islamic Republic of Iran, http://www.iranian.ws/iran_news/ publish/printer_15612.shtml, dated 03/13/2006

(7) http://news.gooya.com/politics/archieves/2006/09/052609print. php, dated 09/07/2006

BAHMAN AGHAI DIBA

-B.A. Political Sciences ,Faculty of Law and Political Sciences, **Tehran University**.

-M.A. International Relations, Center for Graduate **International Studies**, Tehran University.

-Ph.D. International Law (the Law of the Seas), Faculty of Law, **Delhi University**.

Occupations and experiences :

- **World Resources Company**, Consultant in International Affairs

- **Dr. Shirin O. Entezari & Assoc**. (International Law Firm acting in Iran, Turkmenistan, Azerbaijan), Managing partner of the Tehran Office

- **Legal Department**, Iranian Ministry of Foreign Affairs, International law expert, Contacts negotiator, Law of the Sea Expert

Second Secretary in charge of International and Economic affairs, Special Liaison Officer with the Office of the Non-aligned Movement's Affairs, Iranian Embassy (accredited for Nepal, Burma, and Vietnam), New Delhi.

- Liaison Officer, **Asian-African Legal Consultative Organization (AALCO)**, New Delhi, India

Member of the Iranian Delegations to the **United Nations General Assembly** sessions, including the sixth committee (Legal Affairs)

- Member of the Iranian Delegation to **IRAN-IRAQ Peace Talks**, under the supervision of the UN Secretary General, **New York** and **Geneva** (1988)

- Representative of Iran in the International Conference for Revision of IMO Convention on the Civil Liability for Oil Pollution Damage (CLC) and the Convention of International Compensation Fund, Jakarta **(Indonesia)**1984

- Member of the Iranian Delegations to AALCO Annual Sessions in **New Delhi (India), Katmandu (Nepal), and Nairobi (Kenya)**

- Member of the Iranian Delegation to London for Negotiations on Damages to Embassy premises in London and Tehran 1987

- Working with the Office of **United Nations High Commissioner for Refugees**.

- Working with the **United Nations Information Office** in Tehran.

Publications in English:

-Law and Politics of the Caspian Sea 2006

- FAQ about the Nuclear Case of Iran, 2007

- Problems of Iran: How not to govern, 2006

Translation from English into Persian:

-**Black's Law Dictionary**, Published by Ghangedanesh Publications, Tehran, 1999

- **The International Law of the Sea,** by R R Churchill and A V Lowe, Manchester University Press, Published five times in Persian, and the selected textbook for the Law of the Sea in post graduate courses on the law of the sea. The last edition published in 2005.

- **A Modern Introduction to the International Law**, By Professor Akhurst, Published by the Iranian Bureau for International Legal Services, a university textbook for the undergraduate students of the international law, Tehran, 1997.

- **Dictionary of International Law**, By Robert Bledsoe and Boczek, Published by Ghangedanesh Publications, Tehran, 1998.

- **International law governing Communications and Information**, compiled by Edward W. Ploman, International Institute of Communications, Ghangedanesh Publications, Tehran, 200

- **The Foreign Policy of the USSR**, Tehran, 1986

-**Human rights**, published by the Office of the United Nations in Tehran, 2000

Other works:

- **The Law and Politics of the Caspian Sea in the 21st Century**, [in English] The positions and views of the Coastal states, IBEX Publishers, Bethesda, Maryland, 2003.

- **The Rise and Fall of the Pahlavi Dynasty** [in English], translation of the Memoirs of General Hussein Fardoust, Tehran, 1995, Institute for political Studies and Researches

- **Collection of 12 Articles Concerning Law of The Sea** and Iranian Problems, including the legal regime of the Caspian Sea, Iran's Position towards innocent passage in the International Straits and Territorial Waters, and the Passage of Military Ships in the Territorial Sea and The Right of Landlocked States, Published by Ghangedanesh Publications, Tehran, 1997.

- **A Terminology of Human Rights**, published by Ghangedanesh Publications, Tehran 1997.

-**Ikhvan Al Muslemin [Muslim Brotherhood] in the Middle East**, Tehran, 1986.

- Many Articles Regarding International Law and relations published in Iranian and international specialized periodicals